THE EVERYTHING

Cocktail Parties and Drinks Book

Dear Reader:

If you are reading this letter, then I know that you are a person who chooses to live juicy. I predict that you have a passion for life, for good food and drink. Most importantly, you have the desire to celebrate life and cultivate friendships with other people.

Hosting a cocktail party can be intimidating to most, but as you read the wonderful ideas and guidelines in this book, my only hope is that you feel a shot or two of inspiration in your veins to give you the confidence to step into the stylish world of cocktail party entertaining.

Other books will tell you that there are no rules for hosting a cocktail party. I disagree. I believe that there's a tried-and-true formula that you can follow in order to throw very successful cocktail parties. So what are you waiting for? Steal some quiet moments, curl up with *The Everything® Cocktail Parties and Drinks Book*, and then jot down the first ideas that pop into your head. If you need a jump-start, then by all means, feel free to e-mail me at *Cheryl@misscharming.com*.

Cheers!

Cheryl Charming

THE EVERYTHING®

COCKTAIL PARTIES AND DRINKS BOOK

The ultimate guide to creating
colorful concoctions, fabulous finger foods,
and the perfect setting

Cheryl Charming

Adams Media
Avon, Massachusetts

To my mother, Babs Smith, for her encouragement and support

Publishing Director: Gary M. Krebs
Associate Managing Editor: Laura Daly
Associate Copy Chief:
Brett Palana-Shanahan
Acquisitions Editor: Kate Burgo
Development Editors:
Karen Johnson Jacot, Jessica LaPointe
Associate Production Editor: Casey Ebert

Director of Manufacturing: Susan Beale
Associate Director of Production: Michelle Roy Kelly
Cover Design: Paul Beatrice, Matt LeBlanc
Layout and Graphics: Colleen Cunningham,
Holly Curtis, Erin Dawson, Sorae Lee

An Everything® Series Book.
Everything® and everything.com® are registered trademarks of F+W Publications, Inc.

Published by Adams Media, an F+W Publications Company
57 Littlefield Street, Avon, MA 02322 U.S.A.
www.adamsmedia.com

ISBN: 1-59337-390-2
Printed in Canada.

J I H G F E D C B A

Library of Congress Cataloging-in-Publication Data
Charming, Cheryl.
The everything cocktail parties and drinks book : the ultimate guide to creating colorful
concoctions, fabulous finger foods, and the perfect setting / Cheryl Charming.
p. cm. -- (An everything series book)
Includes bibliographical references and index.
ISBN 1-59337-390-2
1. Cocktails. 2. Appetizers. 3. Entertaining. I. Title. II. Series: Everything series.
TX951.C467 2005
641.8'74--dc22
2005017396

This book is available at quantity discounts for bulk purchases.
For information, call 1-800-872-5627.

Contents

Acknowledgments

Major thanks to all the talented people at Adams Media, with special thanks to my project editor, Kate Burgo, and my development editor, Karen Johnson Jacot.

Specific thanks to Dewana Falks and Kate Mansfield for providing a budget for me to host a multitude of themed parties over the years. I would also like to thank my creative sisters, Carolyn and Charlie, for letting me bounce ideas off them. In addition, I thank the ingenious minds of my six nieces, Carly, Mackensey, Leslie, Alex, Meagan, and Tori. Sometimes simple perspectives can turn out to be the most creative.

My continued gratitude is extended to my friends in the cocktail industry for their help, support, and ideas: Mark Hastings, of *www.barproducts.com*; Pål Løberg, of The Webtender (at *www.webtender.com*); Robert Hess, of Drinkboy.com; Toby Ellis, of BarMagic (at *www.barmagic.com*); Dean Serneels, of Flairco.com; Scott Young, of ExtremeBartending.com; and the most famous bartender in NYC, Dale DeGroff, of KingCocktail.com.

Introduction

Believe it or not, the social cocktail party, as we know it today, has not been around very long. If it weren't for Prohibition (the law of the land from 1919 to 1933) and the birth of Hollywood's motion picture industry, many believe that the cocktail party would have never been born.

Imagine what Prohibition must have been like. For centuries upon centuries, all kinds of alcohol—beer, wine, and hard spirits—had been a part of people's everyday life. Then, in 1919, the manufacturing, sale, and import/export of alcohol were suddenly banned in all of the United States, all Canadian provinces, and in the entire country of Finland. I bet there were a lot of vacations taken south of the border!

From the mid-1800s to 1918, in bright cities across America, you could stroll into a saloon and order up a Manhattan, Cuba Libre, or Singapore Sling, among many others. At the same time, many anti-alcohol organizations were formed because people believed that the constant rise of crime was the direct result of alcohol consumption. This battle of the booze was fought for many years until finally on October 28, 1919, the U.S. Constitution was amended to include the Eighteenth Amendment, the legislation behind Prohibition. It took effect on January 16, 1920. The fine for selling alcohol was $1,000 or six months in jail. Can you imagine the New Year's Eve party on December 31, 1919? Or better yet, the party on January 15?

It doesn't take a genius to figure out what happens when you tell someone that they can't have something. It's just human nature to want it even more! The buzzwords of the time included *bootlegging, speakeasy, bathtub gin, home brewing, moonshine, organized crime, smuggling, black market, flasks,* and *gangsters.* Saloons tried to survive by substituting gambling and prostitution for the forbidden alcohol, but the cold hard fact was that people wanted to drink. After all, they had been able to drink for their whole lives already. This is why the underground clubs and bars called speakeasies were able to flourish. Can you believe that there were over 100,000 speakeasies in New York alone? Cocktails became all the rage, and flappers took the stage.

Finally, under the presidency of Franklin D. Roosevelt in 1933, Prohibition was repealed and America was no longer a dry nation. (Mississippi was the exception, remaining dry until 1966.) Swing and jazz clubs swept the nation, and Hollywood's silver screen glamorized cocktails in full style. Who can forget Humphrey Bogart in *Casablanca,* the Rat Pack, and all those bombshell starlets sipping from elegant cocktail glasses while wearing glamorous cocktail dresses?

By the 1950s, women were quite accustomed to entertaining in their homes, and lo and behold, the cocktail party truly came into its own. This was by far the most popular cocktail party decade to date. Combined with new household-appliance technology, the war-free times created a perfect recipe for swanky social entertaining.

Sadly, the cocktail party fizzled out from the 1960s to the 1980s, but by the 1990s an interest in quality in food, drink, and home improvement flourished across the nation, and the cocktail party was back in fashion. Home entertaining became popular again for lots of occasions. People not only wanted to show off their latest home reno- vations, they wanted to show that they knew a thing or two about cool cocktails and swell food.

Today, while experiencing a strong economy, vogue cocktail party hosts are stepping into the stylish world of cocktail party entertaining. The modern-day cocktail party has no limits. It can be swell and small or awesomely big. One thing that is for sure, it's all about celebrating life. And what better to toast than life?

chapter 1

Cocktail Party and Drink-Mixing Basics

Hosting a cocktail party is about bringing people together. If you are the one chosen to host a social gathering and feel a little weak in the knees about it, then this chapter is for you. Sit down and take a deep breath. Soon you'll see that there's really nothing to stress over once you've learned the basics.

Cocktail Party Creed

Raise your right hand and say, "People are what makes a cocktail party." This is the first rule to remember at all times. The number one mistake a host is likely to make is focusing too much on the minor details of a party. If you remember only one thing from this chapter, remember this: Cocktail parties are about conversations, connecting, laughing, and feeling good. Your job is to create an environment where people can relax and where the natural thing to do is enjoy themselves. To make this kind of a five-star cocktail party, you need to supply five ingredients: drink, food, music, ambiance, and amusement.

The first step is to buy a notebook to keep all of your thoughts and ideas organized. Don't be afraid to jot down anything to get started or to insert any ideas you might find in a magazine. Next, you must seek answers to the following questions to determine some basic factors in your planning:

- What or who is this party for?
- Approximately how many people will be invited?
- What is your budget?

ESSENTIAL

You might think that you can remember everything when planning a cocktail party, but even the best of the best carry around a notebook of some kind. The pages of the notebook will go through many ripped-out, chicken-scratched stages, but don't worry. This is what everyone goes through when beginning the creative process.

What or Who Is This Party For?

There are many reasons to host a cocktail party. You might give one for friends and family or for office coworkers. You might want to do networking, or put on a singles bash, or celebrate a birthday, anniversary, raise, retirement, new job, or housewarming. Your party could precede an event like the ballet or a concert. It's important to keep in mind at all times the reason for the event because this will light-speed you back to reality when you are lost in the cocktail party–planning jungle of drinks and food and music, oh my!

After you are clear about what or who the cocktail party is for, you can decide on a theme. Please understand that the traditional idea of a theme is not necessary, so don't feel pressured to come up with one. An invitation that simply describes a "cocktail party" is fine. That's a theme in its own right. The reason you must know who or what the party is for is that you will want to cater it accordingly.

Approximately How Many People Will Be Invited?

Cocktail parties can range in size from ten to ten thousand guests. It's very important to know approximately how many people will be invited because this number is the basis of the math you will have to do for everything related to the party. How else will you be able to calculate the amount of food and drink and the number of invitations, napkins, glasses, and so on? So make a list, check it twice, and always invite the naughty and the nice for a memorable party.

FACT

A good cocktail party will have somewhere between fifteen to forty people and will last two to three hours in order to keep the energy and conversation levels up. Remember that the first hour allows time for the fashionably late to arrive. It's best to invite more people than you plan to show up because 20 to 30 percent usually will not be able to make it. In addition, make sure that you try to invite many different personalities to create interest. There is no perfect time for a cocktail party; it's all up to you.

After the guest list is established, you have to decide on invitations. Invitations should reach guests two weeks before the cocktail party, so put this task at the top of your list. There are resources for cocktail party invitations in Appendix A. You have many other options, including making the invitations yourself, having a local printer design them, finding a cool card shop in your area, or asking a friend with graphic design skills to help out.

What Is Your Budget?

Lastly, you will have to determine your budget. This is a major guideline for the decisions you will have to make for the party. Knowing your budget gives you an idea of what's possible. So what's your budget? Do you have a sky-is-the-limit budget? I-can-afford-a-little-splurge budget? Or do you have champagne-taste-on-a-beer-budget budget? You'll find that it's a great help from the beginning to be honest and up front about the ching-ching.

The Drinks

The drinks are the first cocktail party essential. After all, it is called a cocktail party. If cocktail parties are all about people, then cocktails are all about lubricating the conversations. By all means, you want to get a drink in a guest's hand as soon as you can because this puts them at ease. Guests are often introverted and self-conscious when arriving at a social event, and the glass gives them something to do with at least one hand.

FACT

Forget the full bar unless you are using a caterer, and remember that the bigger the party, the fewer drink choices you should provide. If you've ever attended a big art-gallery cocktail party, you know that only white wine and bottled water are served. The next step would be to add a beer, then a specialty cocktail. The average thrown-at-home cocktail party will have a beer, a wine, a specialty cocktail, and bottled water.

Decide on a specialty cocktail from this book for your party. You can even change the name of the drink to suit your party. If you decide not to hire a bartender, you can supply everything needed and allow guests to make their own cocktails. Print out the recipe directions for display in a standing picture frame. Make sure that you provide everything they will need to make the drink. Keep in mind that a self-service bar can get a little messy.

Bartending

Having a bartender can really make a party. It's always great to know a few good bartenders around your city in case you need one for a party. If you don't know one, then ask around. Another idea is to call your local bartending school and ask about one of their graduates. These economical bartenders are very anxious and excited for the chance to tend bar for you. For a Tom Cruise–type "Flair Bartender" in your area, inquire at the Flair Bartenders Association (FBA) at *www.barflair.org*. There are 6,000 Flair Bartender members on that Web site.

Bar Setup Ideas

There are a few ways that you can set up a bar. Of course, if you already have a bar in your home, then you're all set. If you plan to hire a bartender and have a bar/counter area over your kitchen sink, then this is perfect. The bartender can use the sink for ice, and guests can walk up to the bar. If you do not have a stationary place for a bar, then make one with a table and then a smaller table, like a coffee table, on top. All of this can be covered with linens. One idea that works really well is a self-service beer and wine station. Put the beer and white wine on ice, provide the glasses, and let guests help themselves. Make sure you always have some nonalcoholic still or sparkling water on ice, too.

Calculating Amounts

You never know what guests will drink. But when alcohol is free, beggars can't be choosers, so guests are usually satisfied with what you serve. Guests at a cocktail party will drink about two drinks each. One bottle of wine holds four glasses, and a 750 ml bottle of liquor will give you around twenty-five shots of alcohol. You will also need about half a pound of ice per person. Make sure you can keep extra ice in a cooler for backup. You need to know the number of guests to expect to calculate the amount of booze to buy. You also decide what to serve so you can calculate the amounts. If you decide to have a specialty drink, count on every person to try it at least once.

The Food

Food is the second cocktail party essential. There are a lot of great recipes for you to try in Chapters 13, 14, and 15. Try to choose one or two and stick with those. There's no need to serve more than that.

ESSENTIAL

For a stress-free cocktail party, don't be a slave to your oven. Choose recipes that can be made and served without having to be constantly warmed. A good host should be spending time with guests, not in the kitchen. The very best cocktail foods are finger foods that require no plate or utensils. They can be skewered or kabobbed with frilly toothpicks or bamboo.

The Presentation

Once you've decided on the food you'd like to serve, it's time to think about how to present it. You have two options: to present foods at their food station, or use butler service. Butler service is a classy touch that involves hiring a person or two to walk around offering trays of yummy finger nibbles to your guests. This method can save you money on food, but you usually lose that savings in what you pay the hired help. Alternately, you can set up a food station—a table or buffet where food is presented—and your guests can help themselves.

Setting out food on platters is fine, but to add a professional touch, use some sturdy boxes and linens to create different heights. First, place linens of some kind on the table to create a skirt. Then place the different-sized boxes on the table, drape linens over them, and then scrunch the linens all over. Place your platters of food accordingly and add little folded food labels. If you do not have linens or tablecloths, you can use the paper tablecloths you find at party stores. Just stick with black or white. It's also acceptable to place food on trays all over the room. Don't forget the extras that might be needed, like napkins, plates, or utensils. If you choose to use plastic or paper plates and utensils, buy clear or black.

FACT

You can find perfectly fine serving platters, chafing dishes, linens, and lots of other items you will need for your food presentation table at local thrift stores. Try the thrift stores that are in the wealthier neighborhoods first for the best selection. You will be amazed at what you will find. It's a great way to start building an entertaining collection.

Doing the Math

Guests at a cocktail party will eat around six bites of food per hour. In the first hour, people arrive late. The second hour is the peak hour, and in the third hour they are winding down and getting ready to leave. Although you never can predict exactly how much food will be needed, a good average is about ten bites per person for the entire party. So take the number of people expected and do the math. Make as much as your budget will allow. Don't worry if you run out in the third hour—it's a sign of a great party.

The Music

The third cocktail party essential, music, is a major moodsetter for your party. Find appropriate music for the type of cocktail party you plan to host. Most people have a stereo or sound system for playing CDs. If you don't, then be sure to borrow one from a friend or rent one because music is a must. Make sure that you set the system on repeat so that it will be maintenance-free for the party. Hiring live entertainment is another option. Just make sure that the band will play music through their system during breaks. You don't want one moment without music—until the party is over, that is, and then you turn the music off as a hint to guests.

The Ambiance

Setting the mood and tone for a cocktail party is very important. However, this is the area where hosts tend to go overboard. Try to refrain from really decorating the place unless it's with light.

You can never have too many candles. Make sure all are protected in containers to prevent accidents. Setting out lightly scented tea lights in cocktail glasses is nice. And don't forget to stock up on little white lights during the holiday season, because you can use them around the bar, food area, and many other places. If the outside entrance permits, it's nice to have a couple of Tiki torches burning. Dimmer switches and low-watt lightbulbs are great ways to create tone as well.

You may want to clear the room of large furniture. The idea is to create space where your guests can mingle. Hide furniture in a bedroom, or, if weather permits, set it up outside to create more space for guests. You might make it the smoking area. For the most part, guests at cocktail parties stand, rather than sit, so give them room.

The Amusement

There's no doubt about it; people love the element of fun. Most believe that the amusement is the glue that bonds all other elements of a cocktail party. In accordance with human nature, most people are apprehensive and uncomfortable at social gatherings, but the amusement breaks the ice and gives guests something in common.

You'll have to determine the level of amusement that is appropriate for your cocktail party. This will depend on the type of cocktail party that you are hosting. Remember that an amusement doesn't have to be outrageous. It can be simple and subtle, like the way food or drink is presented. The goal is to create an environment in which people are surprised and delighted.

Keep in mind that some amusements fall under the category of entertainment, and as everyone knows, you have to pay for entertainment. Most hosts don't think twice about the cost, because they know that this will be the extra special thing that guests will keep talking about for a long time. Here are a few ideas:

- **Disposable cameras:** People love photos, so place disposable cameras around, and guests can snap their own. Have special containers for the cameras with a clipboard and pen tied to them and a note asking guests to provide their e-mail address if they'd like to see the photos. There are many places on the Web where you can upload the photos for free to share them with people (as described in Appendix A). When you get the photos developed, make sure that you ask for them on CD so you've got digital files to upload.

- **Polaroid photos:** Why not hire a friendly face to work the room, taking Polaroid photos to give your guests instant souvenirs of your cocktail party?

- **Clever nametags:** If your party guests have never met each other, provide nametags for everyone at the door. Instead of having them just say, "Hi, my name is _____," add a special suggestion below the name that says, "Ask me about _____." Guests can fill in the "ask me about" blank with an interest or unusual hobby. This is a great icebreaker and conversation starter. You can have these name tags made especially for you at your local printer. Just tell them what you want the labels to say, and specify that you'd like to have them printed on crack-n-peel paper (sticker paper).

- **Jukebox:** Rent a jukebox and let guests have fun choosing their own music.
- **Fortune-teller:** Hiring a fortune-teller may seem old hat, but deep down, people really like it. Try to provide a mysterious area for the psychic, with dim lights and translucent hangings, so that guests can barely see what's going on. This creates a buzz about the room.
- **Celebrity look-alike:** Live actors are the best. They add such life to a party that you will have guests talking for days. You can call up your local entertainment company, ask around, or put a flyer up around your local college drama department.
- **Live musical entertainment:** Depending on the size of your cocktail party, you can have a one-, two-, or three-piece band —or more— to entertain your guests.
- **Artist:** The most popular idea is to hire a caricature artist. People simply love to see themselves turned into a cartoon.
- **Color:** Making your cocktail party a "color" cocktail party is fun. Guests show up in a certain color, and the drinks can be that color as well. People love the whole concept of color.

chapter 2

Martinis for the Adventurous

Itsy Bitsy Teenie Weenie Yellow Polka Dot Martini

Makes 1 drink

½ ounce dark chocolate
1 ounce Limoncello
1 ounce raspberry-flavored vodka
3 ounces lemonade

Melt the dark chocolate in the microwave. Carefully dip your finger in the chocolate, then make polka dots on the inside of a martini glass. Set the glass in the freezer for a minute to harden the chocolate. Pour the other ingredients into a shaker tin of ice. Shake, then strain into the glass.

· ·

Melontini

Makes 1 drink

½ ounce dark chocolate
2 ounces Southern Comfort
1 ounce crème de noya
2 ounces orange juice

The popular comedian Gallagher, who is known for smashing a watermelon with a sledgehammer at the end of his shows, had his first harvest of his own version of the fruit, the "Gallagher Watermelon," on June 26, 2004. Look for it at your local grocer.

Melt the dark chocolate in the microwave. Carefully dip your finger in the chocolate, then make polka dots on the inside of a martini glass. Set the glass in the freezer for a minute to harden the chocolate. Pour the rest of the ingredients into a shaker tin of ice. Shake, and strain into the prepped martini glass. The drink looks exactly like a red watermelon with seeds. Surprisingly, it tastes like watermelon, too!

I Dream of Genie Martini

Makes 6 drinks

1½ cups cherry-flavored vodka
3 cups pink lemonade
1 ounce grenadine for color
Large chunk of dry ice

If you can't find cherry vodka, you can make your own (as described in Chapter 10). You can also drop a few cherry Jolly Ranchers into a bottle of vodka.

Prepare these martinis ahead of time by pouring the first three ingredients into a large serving pitcher, then refrigerate. (The ultimate presentation would be to use a tall genie bottle–type container and maybe hot-glue some jewels from the craft store onto the bottle.) When you are ready to serve, drop in a large chunk of dry ice to activate your Genie Martini mixture, then pour into martini glasses. Another way to prep is to refrigerate your liquid ingredients ahead of time.

Goin' Coconutini

Makes 1 drink

1 tablespoon light corn syrup
Shredded coconut
2 ounces coconut rum
3 ounces white (clear) cranberry juice

Pour the corn syrup onto a saucer or small plate, and put the shredded coconut on another. Dip the rim of the glass first in the corn syrup, then in the shredded coconut. Pour the next two ingredients into a shaker tin of ice. Shake, and strain into the coconut-rimmed glass.

Peaches and Creamtini

Makes 1 drink

1½ ounces orange-flavored vodka
1½ ounces peach schnapps
2 ounces orange juice
Splash of half-and-half

Pour all the ingredients into a shaker tin of ice. Shake, then strain into a martini glass. If you prefer a creamier martini, use less orange juice and more half-and-half. Mandarin-flavored vodka tastes nice with this drink as well. If you prefer more peach flavor, add more schnapps than vodka.

. . . .

White Chocolatini

Makes 1 drink

1½ ounces vanilla vodka
1 ounce Godiva White Chocolate Liqueur
2 ounces half-and-half
White chocolate shavings

Pour the first three ingredients into a shaker tin of ice. Shake, then strain into a martini glass. Sprinkle the white chocolate shavings on top. If you are a real chocoholic, use chocolate vodka in place of the vanilla. You should be able to find a bottle at your local liquor store.

Blue Velvetini

Makes 1 drink

1 ounce light rum
1 ounce blue curaçao
1 ounce blueberry schnapps
2 ounces white (clear) cranberry juice
Sugar
Blue food coloring

Mix the sugar with just enough food coloring to make it blue, and put sugar in a saucer or small plate. Wet the rim of a martini glass with water and dip the rim in the blue sugar. Pour the first four ingredients into a shaker tin of ice. Shake, then strain into the glass.

· ·

Pink Cadillactini

Makes 1 drink

1 ounce vanilla vodka
½ ounce Galliano
½ ounce white crème de cacao
1/8 ounce grenadine
3 ounces half-and-half or milk

This is the perfect drink for a Girls' Night in Pink party. Or, if you're throwing an eighties party and looking for a specialty martini to serve, this one fits the bill.

Pour all the ingredients into a shaker tin of ice. Shake until cold and frothy, then strain into a martini glass. You can also use plain vodka or substitute chocolate-flavored. If you don't like the subtle taste of licorice, omit the Galliano and add more crème de cacao.

Good Karmatini

Makes 1 drink

1 ounce light rum
1 ounce raspberry liqueur
1 ounce melon liqueur
1 ounce pineapple juice
1 ounce sweet-n-sour mix

Pour all the ingredients into a shaker tin of ice. Shake, then strain into a martini glass. If you don't like rum, substitute vodka. Flavored rums and vodkas are not good with this recipe, because they will make it taste too sweet.

Green-Eyed Blondtini

Makes 1 drink

1 ounce melon liqueur
1 ounce banana liqueur
1 ounce Irish cream liqueur
2 ounces half-and-half or milk

Pour all the ingredients into a shaker tin of ice. Shake, and strain into a martini glass. If you want to raise the alcohol level of this drink, add 1 ounce of vodka or rum. If not, then leave it as a simple Green-Eyed Blondtini.

Black Martini

Makes 1 drink

1 ounce Blavod black vodka
1 ounce raspberry liqueur
1 ounce triple sec
2 ounces sweet-n-sour mix

This is a fantabulous martini for a color-themed party. Guests can wear black, but if you want to think outside the black box, turn all the lights off and hand guests a flashlight at the door.

Pour all the ingredients into a shaker tin of ice. Shake, then strain into a martini glass. If you like, serve this black drink in a glass with a white-sugared rim. If you cannot locate Blavod black vodka, replace the triple sec with blue curaçao. The raspberry liqueur and blue curaçao together look almost black.

Lucky Charmartini

Makes 1 drink

1 ounce Tequila Rose
1 ounce white crème de menthe
3 ounces milk
Marshmallows from Lucky Charms cereal

Pour the first three ingredients into a shaker tin of ice. Swirl around to chill. Strain into a martini glass, then sprinkle your choice of Lucky Charms marshmallows on top. If you want, throw in some toasted oats—it will taste almost like having breakfast because this drink is "magically delicious!"

Caramel Appletini

Makes 1 drink

2 ounces apple-flavored vodka
1 ounce Apple Pucker Schnapps
1 ounce Dooley's caramel liqueur
1 ounce half-and-half or milk

Pour all the ingredients into a shaker tin of ice. Shake, then strain into a martini glass. Some people like to add butterscotch schnapps to this recipe in place of the caramel liqueur. Try using half of each for a slight change of taste. You can also use plain vodka.

* *

Southern Hospitality Martini

Makes 1 drink

2 ounces Southern Comfort
2 ounces peach schnapps

Southern Comfort is often mistaken for bourbon, but it's really a liqueur. It has a bourbon base that is infused with peaches and apricots. It was invented in 1870 by a bartender in New Orleans.

Fill a shaker tin with ice and pour in the Southern Comfort and peach schnapps. Shake for about 20 seconds, then strain into a martini glass. These two liqueurs combine to create a great balance of flavors. Make sure that you get the mixture very cold when shaking.

Honeymoon Suitetini

Makes 1 drink

1 ounce Irish cream liqueur
1 ounce hazelnut liqueur
½ ounce coffee liqueur
½ ounce honey
2 ounces half-and-half or milk
2 chocolate Kisses candies

Pour all the liquid ingredients into a shaker tin of ice. Shake, and strain into a martini glass. Unwrap the two chocolate Kisses and drop into the martini. If you do not like the nutty flavor of the hazelnut liqueur, simply omit it and add an extra ½ ounce of each of the other liqueurs.

God Bless Texastini

Makes 1 drink

1 ounce gold tequila
1 ounce Tequila Rose
1½ ounces orange juice
1½ ounces pineapple juice

Pour all the ingredients into a shaker tin of ice. Shake, then strain into a martini glass. If you would like a creamy version of this drink, add a splash of half-and-half. If you don't much like tequila, you can replace it with vanilla vodka, which will give the drink a Creamsicle taste.

Death by Chocolatini

Makes 1 drink

½ ounce chocolate
1 strawberry
Chocolate syrup
1½ ounces vanilla vodka
1½ ounces chocolate liqueur
2 ounces half-and-half

Although chocolate may not be an actual aphrodisiac, it does contain phenylethyl-amine, a natural substance that is reputed to stimulate the same reaction in the body as falling in love.

Melt the chocolate in a microwave. Dip the strawberry in the chocolate, then cool briefly in the freezer to harden. Swirl chocolate syrup inside a martini glass, then put in the freezer. Pour the vodka, chocolate liqueur, and half-and-half into a shaker tin of ice. Shake, then strain into the cold chocolate-coated glass. Garnish the rim with the chocolate-dipped strawberry.

Almond Joytini

Makes 1 drink

1 ounce coconut rum
1 ounce amaretto
1 ounce crème de cacao
2 ounces half-and-half

Pour all the ingredients into a shaker tin of ice. Shake, then strain into a martini glass. This martini tastes just like an Almond Joy candy bar. If you're not a nutty person, leave out the amaretto and add an additional half ounce each of coconut rum and crème de cacao—now it's a Mounds bar.

Upside-Down Pineapple Martini

Makes 1 drink

1 ounce vanilla vodka
1 ounce Irish cream liqueur
1 ounce butterscotch schnapps
2 ounces pineapple juice
Maraschino cherry

Pour the first four ingredients into a shaker tin of ice. Shake, then strain into a martini glass. Drop in the cherry, and you've made an Upside-Down Pineapple Martini without even turning on the oven. In a pinch, you can use regular vodka in place of the vanilla flavored.

Tootsie Rolltini

Makes 1 drink

1 ounce coffee liqueur
1 ounce dark crème de cacao
3 ounces orange juice

Pour all the ingredients into a shaker tin of ice. Shake, then strain into a martini glass. If you find yourself wondering about this martini, rest assured that as weird as it sounds, it does taste exactly like a Tootsie Roll. Taste the two together and compare—if you dare.

chapter 3

Margarita Madness

Tequila Mockingbird Margarita

Makes 1 drink

1½ ounces tequila
½ ounce green crème de menthe
Juice from half a lime
3 ounces sweet-n-sour mix
Lime wheel and kosher salt

Making frozen drinks can be tricky sometimes. Just keep in mind that if it's not thick enough, all you have to do is throw some more ice cubes into the blender. If it's too thick, just add a little more sweet-n-sour mix.

Rub the lime wheel around the rim of a margarita glass, then dip the rim in kosher salt. Pour the tequila, green crème de menthe, lime juice, and sweet-n-sour mix into a blender with a cup of ice. Blend until smooth. Pour into the glass and garnish with the lime wheel. Gold tequila can be used instead.

Strawberry Mojitorita

Makes 1 drink

Juice from half a lime
5 mint leaves
4 large strawberries
1½ ounces tequila
½ ounce triple sec
Sweet-n-sour mix
Lime wheel and kosher salt

Rub the lime wheel around the rim of a margarita glass, and dip the rim in kosher salt. Reserve one mint leaf and half a strawberry; muddle the lime juice and the rest of the mint and strawberries with a muddler or a wooden spoon. Pour mixture into the glass and fill with ice. Add the tequila and triple sec, then fill with sweet-n-sour mix. Garnish with the lime wheel, strawberry half, and mint leaf.

White Sangriarita

Makes 1 drink

1½ ounces tequila
1 ounce white wine
5 ounces sweet-n-sour mix
Lime wheel, orange wheel, lemon wheel,
*   maraschino cherry, and kosher salt*

Sangria comes from Spain and has grown to be a very popular party drink. It is typically made from red wine, but white wine Sangria has become very popular in recent years. Spain meets Mexico in this recipe.

Rub the lime wheel around the rim of a margarita glass, then dip the rim in kosher salt. Pour the tequila, white wine, and sweet-n-sour mix into a blender with a cup of ice. Blend until smooth. Pour into the glass and garnish top of drink with fruit slices and cherry. Gold tequila can be substituted.

Between the Hotel Sheets Margarita

Makes 1 drink

1½ ounces gold tequila
½ ounce Grand Marnier
Juice from half a lime
3 ounces sweet-n-sour mix
Lime wheel and kosher salt

Throughout this chapter, recipes call for a "margarita glass." These come in a variety of shapes and are easy to find in any home or kitchen store. You can substitute any other glass if you don't have a margarita glass.

Rub the lime wheel around the rim of a margarita glass, then dip rim in kosher salt. Pour the tequila, Grand Marnier, lime juice, and sweet-n-sour mix into a blender with a cup of ice. Blend until smooth. Pour into the glass and garnish with the lime wheel. If you prefer, you can combine the liquid ingredients in a shaker and pour over ice for an on-the-rocks version.

Swim-up Bar Margarita

Makes 1 drink

1½ ounces tequila
1 ounce blue curaçao
Juice from half a lime
3 ounces sweet-n-sour mix
Lime wheel and kosher salt

Rub the lime wheel around the rim of a margarita glass, then dip the rim in kosher salt. Pour the tequila, blue curaçao, lime juice, and sweet-n-sour mix into a blender with a cup of ice. Blend until smooth. Pour into the glass and garnish with the lime wheel. Can also be served on the rocks.

· ·

Beer Belly Margarita

Makes 1 drink

1½ ounces tequila
2 ounces Mexican beer
Juice from half a lime
3 ounces sweet-n-sour mix
Lime wheel and kosher salt

The most popular Mexican beers imported to America are Corona, Sol, Tecate, and Dos Equis. They come from the two main Mexican breweries: Grupo Modelo and Cerveceria Cuauhtemoc Moctezuma. Any of those beers is fine for this recipe.

Rub the lime wheel around the rim of a margarita glass, then dip the rim in kosher salt. Pour the tequila, Mexican beer, lime juice, and sweet-n-sour mix into a blender with a cup of ice. Blend until smooth. Pour into the glass and garnish with the lime wheel. Can also be served on the rocks.

Cranberry Cosmorita

Makes 1 drink

1½ ounces tequila
½ ounce triple sec
Juice from half a lime
2 ounces cranberry juice
2 ounces sweet-n-sour mix
Lime wheel and kosher salt

Rub the lime wheel around the rim of a margarita glass, then dip the rim in kosher salt. Pour the tequila, triple sec, lime juice, cranberry juice, and sweet-n-sour mix into a blender with a cup of ice. Blend until smooth. Pour into the glass and garnish with the lime wheel. Can also be served on the rocks.

Lemon Raspberry Rita

Makes 1 drink

1½ ounces gold tequila
½ ounce Chambord
Juice from half a lemon
Lemonade
Lemon wheel and kosher salt

Rub the lemon wheel around the rim of a margarita glass, then dip the rim in kosher salt. Fill glass with ice, then pour in the tequila, Chambord, and lemon juice. Fill glass with lemonade and garnish with the lemon wheel. Can also be served blended.

Hypnotizing Margarita

Makes 1 drink

1½ ounces tequila

1 ounce Hpnotiq

Juice from half a lime

3 ounces sweet-n-sour mix

Lime wheel and kosher salt

Hpnotiq is a liqueur made from triple-distilled vodka, fine cognac, and tropical fruit juices. Its recipe is a family secret that has been handed down from generation to generation. The most alluring thing about it is its ocean-blue color.

Rub the rim of a margarita glass with the lime wheel, then dip the rim in kosher salt. Pour the tequila, Hpnotiq, lime juice, and sweet-n-sour mix into a blender with a cup of ice. Blend until smooth. Pour into the glass and garnish with the lime wheel. Gold tequila can be used instead.

Uno Dos Tres Cuatro Cinco de Mayo Rita

Makes 1 drink

½ ounce tequila

½ ounce triple sec

½ ounce vodka

½ ounce gin

½ ounce rum

Sweet-n-sour mix

Lime wheel and kosher salt

Rub the rim of a margarita glass with the lime wheel, then dip the rim in kosher salt. Fill glass with ice. Pour the tequila, triple sec, vodka, gin, and rum into the glass of ice, then fill with sweet-n-sour mix. Garnish with the lime wheel.

Kiss from a Rosarita

Makes 1 drink

1½ ounces gold tequila
1 ounce Tequila Rose
3 strawberries
3 ounces sweet-n-sour mix
Lime wheel and kosher salt

Tequila Rose is a strawberry-cream liqueur with tequila. It's a slightly tangy, not-too-sweet liqueur that tastes like melted strawberry ice cream. It goes down smooth, as they say.

Rub the rim of a margarita glass with the lime wheel, then dip the rim in kosher salt. Pour the gold tequila, Tequila Rose, strawberries, and sweet-n-sour mix into a blender with a cup of ice. Blend until smooth. Pour into the glass and garnish with the lime wheel. Plain tequila can be used instead.

- -

Anita Rita Now

Makes 1 drink

1½ ounces gold tequila
3/4 ounce triple sec
½ ounce lime juice
8 ounces limeade

Pour the gold tequila into a shot glass. Pour the triple sec and the lime juice into another shot glass. Fill a tall glass with ice, then fill with limeade. Drink the tequila shot, then the lime juice and triple sec, then suck down the limeade. That is the fastest Rita when you need a Rita now!

Tasting Away in Margaritaville

Makes 1 drink

1½ ounces tequila
½ ounce triple sec
2 ounces mango nectar
1 ounce sweet-n-sour mix
Lime wheel and kosher salt

Rub the lime wheel around the rim of a margarita glass, then dip the rim in kosher salt. Pour the tequila, triple sec, mango nectar, and sweet-n-sour mix into a blender with a cup of ice. Blend until smooth. Pour into the glass and garnish with the lime wheel. Gold tequila can be used instead.

Muy Bonita Rita

Makes 1 drink

½ ounce tequila
1½ ounces Licor 43
1 ounce sweet-n-sour mix
1 ounce half-and-half
Lime wheel and a crushed graham cracker

Rub the lime wheel around rim of a margarita glass, then dip the rim in the crushed graham cracker. Pour the tequila, Licor 43, sweet-n-sour mix, and half-and-half into a shaker tin of ice. Shake, then strain into the glass and garnish with a lime wheel.

Le Femme Nikita Rita

Makes 1 drink

1½ ounces gold tequila
1 ounce Limoncello
Juice from half a lemon
3 ounces sweet-n-sour mix
Lemon wheel and kosher salt

Visitors to Italy will be familiar with Limoncello. Invented by Italian monks, this lemon-flavored liqueur is served chilled in the summer months at almost every restaurant.

Rub the lemon wheel around the rim of a margarita glass, then dip the rim in kosher salt. Pour the gold tequila, Limoncello, lemon juice, and sweet-n-sour mix into a blender with a cup of ice. Blend until smooth. Pour into the glass and garnish with the lemon wheel. Can also be served on the rocks.

- -

South of the Peachy Border Rita

Makes 1 drink

1½ ounces tequila
1 ounce peach schnapps
1/8 ounce grenadine
3 ounces sweet-n-sour mix
Lime wheel and kosher salt

Rub the lime wheel around the rim of a margarita glass, then dip the rim in kosher salt. Pour the tequila, peach schnapps, grenadine, and sweet-n-sour mix into a blender with a cup of ice. Blend until smooth. Pour into the glass and garnish with the lemon wheel. Can also be served on the rocks.

Horny Margarita

Makes 1 drink

1 ounce Cointreau

Juice from half a lime

3 ounces sweet-n-sour mix

Lime wheel and kosher salt

1½ ounces Sauza Hornitos 100% agave reposado tequila

Hornitos Reposado tequila is made by the Sauza distillery, founded by Don Cenobio. *Reposado* means "rested," and this tequila must be aged at least two months in wood barrels. Many tequilas are aged in used bourbon barrels.

Rub the lime wheel around the rim of a margarita glass, then dip the rim in kosher salt. Pour the Sauza Hornitos, Cointreau, lime juice, and sweet-n-sour mix into a blender with a cup of ice. Blend until smooth. Pour into the glass and garnish with the lime wheel. Can also be served on the rocks.

Key Lime Pie Margarita

Makes 1 drink

1½ ounces tequila

½ ounce key lime crème liqueur

3 ounces key lime yogurt

Juice from half a lime

Lime wheel, crushed graham cracker, and kosher salt

Rub the lime wheel around the rim of a margarita glass. Dip half the rim in kosher salt and half in graham cracker. Pour the tequila, key lime crème liqueur, key lime yogurt, and lime juice into a blender with a cup of ice. Blend until smooth. Pour into the glass and garnish with the lime wheel.

Three Señoritas Margarita

Makes 1 drink

1½ ounces triple sec
Juice from half a lime
5 ounces sweet-n-sour mix
1 ounce brandy
1 ounce Tequila Rose
1 ounce sherry
3 plastic test tubes

Pour the triple sec, lime juice, and sweet-n-sour mix into a blender with a cup of ice. Blend until smooth, then pour into a margarita glass. Fill the first test tube with brandy, the next with Tequila Rose, and the third with sherry. Stick all three tubes so they stand up in the margarita. Drink the "ladies" at your leisure.

· ·

Tequila Sunrise Margarita

Makes 1 drink

1½ ounces tequila
½ ounce triple sec
1 ounce orange juice
1 ounce sweet-n-sour mix
½ ounce grenadine
Lime wheel and kosher salt

Rub the lime wheel around the rim of a margarita glass, then dip the rim in kosher salt. Pour the tequila, triple sec, orange juice, and sweet-n-sour mix into a blender with a cup of ice. Blend until smooth. Pour the grenadine into the glass, then carefully measure the blended mixture on top. Garnish with the lime wheel.

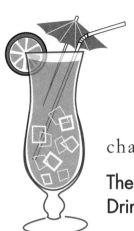

chapter 4

The Hottest Frozen and Tropical Drinks under the Sun

California Dreamin' Creamsicle

Makes 1 drink

1 ounce vanilla vodka
1 ounce coconut rum
½ ounce Galliano
5 ounces orange juice
2 scoops vanilla ice cream
Paper parasol

Pour the vanilla vodka, coconut rum, Galliano, and orange juice into a blender. Add the vanilla ice cream, then blend until creamy. Depending on the size of your ice cream scoops, you may need to add more vanilla ice cream or more orange juice to achieve the right consistency. Pour into a tall glass and garnish with the parasol.

Lulu of a Luau

Makes 1 drink

1 ounce cranberry juice
1 ounce raspberry vodka
1 ounce peach schnapps
1 ounce blue curaçao
2 scoops rainbow sherbet
1 ounce champagne
Fruit of your choice (for garnish)
Paper parasol

Pour the cranberry juice into a tall glass. Pour the vodka, peach schnapps, blue curaçao, and rainbow sherbet into a blender. Blend until smooth. Pour the mixture into the glass, leaving room to add the champagne on top. Garnish with fruit and a paper parasol.

Swirl from Ipanema

Makes 1 drink

1 ounce dark rum
1 ounce coffee liqueur
3 ounces pineapple juice
2 ounces Coco Lopez
Half-and-half
Chocolate syrup
Paper parasol

"The Girl from Ipanema," a song written by Antonio Carlos Jobim, is the most popular bossa nova song to come out of Brazil. "Tall and tan and young and lovely, the girl from Ipanema goes walking, and when she passes each one she passes goes 'A-a-ah!'"

Pour the dark rum, coffee liqueur, and piña colada mix into a blender with a cup of ice. Blend, slowly adding the half-and-half until you achieve a smooth consistency. Swirl the chocolate syrup around the inside of a tall glass, then pour in the drink.

Chocolate Pudding Pop

Makes 1 drink

1 ounce chocolate-flavored vodka
1 ounce coffee liqueur
1 ounce Irish cream liqueur
2 scoops chocolate ice cream
Half-and-half
Chocolate fudge pudding pop

Pour the chocolate-flavored vodka, coffee liqueur, Irish cream liqueur, and ice cream in a blender. Add the half-and-half little by little until a smooth consistency is achieved. Pour into a tall glass and garnish with the chocolate fudge pop. You can substitute the chocolate-flavored vodka with vanilla-flavored.

Copabanana Split

Makes 1 drink

1 ounce vanilla vodka
1 ounce strawberry-flavored vodka
2 ounces half-and-half (or to taste)
1 banana, cut in half lengthwise
2 scoops vanilla ice cream

1 ounce dark crème de cacao
1 ounce strawberry syrup
Whipped cream, nuts,
    and a maraschino cherry

Pour the vodkas and the half-and-half into a blender; add half the banana and the ice cream. Blend until smooth, adding more half-and-half if necessary to achieve desired consistency. Pour the dark crème de cacao into a tall glass, then fill halfway with the blended mixture. Add the strawberry syrup, then continue to fill the glass. Garnish with remaining half banana across the rim, then add whipped cream, nuts, and a cherry.

Tropical Rain Forest

Makes 1 drink

½ ounce lemon vodka
½ ounce cherry rum
½ ounce white tequila
½ ounce blue curaçao
½ ounce melon liqueur

Cranberry juice
Pineapple juice
Orange juice
Paper parasol

Fill a tall glass with ice and pour in the vodka, rum, white tequila, blue curaçao, and melon liqueur. Fill with equal parts of cranberry, pineapple, and orange juice. Garnish with a paper parasol. Experimentation with other flavors of vodka and rum is highly encouraged. You can try raspberry-, strawberry-, cranberry-, or orange-flavored vodka or rum.

Peaches at the Beaches

Makes 1 drink

2 ounces peach schnapps
1 ounce light rum
5 ounces orange juice
½ ounce grenadine
1 peach
Paper parasol

Pour the peach schnapps, light rum, orange juice, grenadine, and half of the peach into a blender with a cup of ice and blend. Add more orange juice if needed. Pour into a tall glass and garnish with remaining peach half, sliced, and a paper parasol.

- -

Screamin' Ice Cream

Makes 1 drink

This adult version of a root beer float tastes just like the ones you had as a kid! This one is by far the most surprising drink you will ever have in your lifetime.

1 ounce Galliano
1 ounce vanilla vodka
1 ounce half-and-half
Cola
Whipped cream

Fill a tall glass with ice and pour in the Galliano, vanilla vodka, and half-and-half. Fill with cola and garnish the top of the drink with whipped cream. This sounds odd, but it's actually good. You can always leave out the vanilla vodka if you prefer a weaker drink.

Tropical Heat Wave

Makes 1 drink

2 ounces mandarin vodka
1 ounce Passoa liqueur
3 ounces mango nectar
2 ounces sweet-n-sour mix
Fruit (for garnish)
Paper parasol

Pour the mandarin vodka, Passoa liqueur, mango nectar, and sweet-n-sour mix into a blender with a cup of ice. Blend until smooth. Pour into a tall glass and garnish with your chosen fruits and the paper parasol. You can substitute your favorite fruit-flavored vodka for the mandarin.

· ·

Latitude Attitude Adjuster

Makes 1 drink

Half a glass of beer (any kind)
Half a glass of orange juice
½ ounce 151 rum
½ ounce amaretto

This drink is a tropical spin-off from the classic boilermaker, which involves dropping a shot of whiskey into a mug of beer. Some people just pour the bourbon in the beer, but the former method is the most popular.

Fill a tall glass with the beer and orange juice. Pour the 151 rum and amaretto into a shot glass. Hold the shot glass in one hand and the tall glass in the other, drop the shot into the glass, then chug the entire drink.

Bermuda Triangle Tea

Makes 1 drink

1 ounce Bermuda Black Seal Rum
1 ounce Bacardi light rum
Florida orange juice
Sweet-n-sour mix
Paper parasol

Fill a tall glass with ice and pour in the Bermuda Black Seal Rum and Bacardi light rum, then fill with equal amounts of Florida orange juice and sweet-n-sour mix. Garnish with a paper parasol. You can replace the light rum with spiced rum if you like.

Watermelon Tidal Wave

Makes 1 drink

1 ounce watermelon schnapps
½ ounce Southern Comfort
½ ounce amaretto
Fill with Mountain Dew

Fill a tall glass with ice and add the watermelon schnapps, Southern Comfort, and amaretto. Fill glass with Mountain Dew and stir. To get more of a kick, add an extra ounce of Southern Comfort. If you do not like amaretto, you can leave it out.

Banana Popsicle

Makes 1 drink

1 ounce Cabana Boy Banana Rum
1 ounce crème de banana
1 ounce simple syrup (page 111)
1 ounce water
Paper parasol

Pour the rum, crème de banana, simple syrup, and water into a blender, and add a cup of cracked ice. Blend until smooth and pour into a glass of your choice. Options at this point include adding more water or ice for your preferred slushiness or adding more simple syrup for a sweeter taste. Garnish with a paper parasol.

• •

Blue Hawaiian Punch

Makes 1 drink

1 ounce light rum
1 ounce coconut rum
1 ounce blue curaçao
1 ounce Coco Lopez
Pineapple juice
Sweet-n-sour mix
Pineapple slice, maraschino cherry, and paper parasol

This tropical libation packs a punch, so be careful. If you'd like to tone it way down, you can leave out the light rum. On the other hand, if you'd like to really punch it up, then replace the light rum with 151 rum.

Fill a tall glass with the light rum, coconut rum, blue curaçao, and Coco Lopez. Add equal parts pineapple juice and sweet-n-sour mix to fill the glass, then stir. Garnish with a pineapple slice and maraschino cherry. If you'd prefer a frozen drink, then simply pour everything into a blender and blend.

Sex with the Captain

Makes 1 drink

2 ounces Captain Morgan Spiced Rum
½ ounce peach schnapps
Cranberry juice
Orange juice
Paper parasol

Fill a tall glass with ice. Pour in the Captain Morgan Spiced Rum and peach schnapps. Fill with equal parts of cranberry and orange juice, then stir. Garnish with a paper parasol. If the Captain Morgan is too spicy for you, then replace one ounce with an equal amount of light rum.

The Big Chill Out

Makes 1 drink

1 ounce 151 rum
1 ounce dark rum
1 ounce blackberry brandy
1 ounce crème de banana
1 ounce Roses lime juice
1 ounce grenadine
Paper parasol

This recipe is a variation of a Rum Runner. It is believed to come from the Florida Keys. The Tiki Bar at Pelican Cove claims to be the inventor and holds a Rum Runner chug-a-lug contest every year.

Pour the 151 rum, dark rum, blackberry brandy, crème de banana, Roses, and grenadine into a blender with 2 cups of ice. Blend until smooth. Taste at this point to determine if you prefer it to be sweeter. To make it sweeter, add a little more grenadine. Garnish with a paper parasol.

Spiked Coconut Brownie

Makes 1 drink

1 ounce coconut rum
1 ounce vanilla vodka
½ ounce hazelnut liqueur
2 scoops chocolate ice cream
1 packet hot cocoa
1 ounce Coco Lopez
Half-and-half
1 ounce shredded coconut

Pour the coconut rum, vanilla vodka, hazelnut liqueur, chocolate ice cream, hot cocoa, and Coco Lopez into a blender. Slowly add the half-and-half until consistency is correct. Pour into a tall glass and sprinkle the shredded coconut on top.

Chocolate Monkey

Makes 1 drink

1 ounce coffee liqueur
1 ounce crème de banana
1 ounce light rum
1 ounce chocolate syrup
5 ounces half-and-half
1 banana

Serve with a chocolate banana. Peel a banana, insert a popsicle stick in the bottom, and place in the freezer. Melt some chocolate in the microwave, and dip the hardened banana in the chocolate. Return to the freezer.

Pour the coffee liqueur, crème de banana, light rum, chocolate syrup, and half-and-half into a blender with the banana and a cup of ice. Blend well, adding more ice or half-and-half as needed to achieve a smooth consistency. If you prefer more of a chocolate flavor, add more chocolate syrup.

Girl Scout Cookie in a Blender

Makes 1 drink

1 ounce dark crème de cacao
½ ounce Frangelico
½ ounce Irish cream liqueur
½ ounce butterscotch schnapps
½ ounce vanilla vodka

¼ ounce cinnamon schnapps
2 scoops vanilla ice cream
Large chocolate chip cookie
Whipped cream and a straw

Pour the dark crème de cacao, Frangelico, Irish cream liqueur, butterscotch schnapps, vanilla vodka, cinnamon schnapps, and ice cream into a blender. Blend until smooth. Pour into a tall glass and place the cookie on top. Add whipped cream on top of the cookie, then stick a fat straw through the cookie into the glass.

- -

Paradise under a Coconut Tree

Makes 1 drink

2 ounces coconut rum
1 ounce light rum
3 ounces Coco Lopez
3 ounces pineapple juice
2 ounces half-and-half

¼ ounce vanilla extract
Coconut
Hacksaw or band saw
Paper parasol

Make a coconut cup by cutting the top off a coconut with the saw. Pour the coconut rum, light rum, Coco Lopez, pineapple juice, half-and-half, and vanilla extract into a blender with a cup of ice. Blend until smooth. Add more ice or half-and-half as needed, then pour into the coconut cup.

chapter 5

Striped Slurps and Sips

American Beauty

Makes 1 drink

1 ounce light rum
4 ounces strawberry daiquiri mix
1 ounce coconut rum
4 ounces piña colada mix
½ ounce blue curaçao
Star fruit, cut into slices

Pour the light rum and strawberry daiquiri mix into a blender with a cup of ice. Blend until smooth, then pour into a tall glass to fill halfway. Pour the coconut rum and piña colada mix into the blender with a cup of ice. Blend until smooth, and fill the glass. Float the blue curaçao on top, then garnish the rim with a slice of star fruit.

Candy Corn

Makes 1 drink

1/3 ounce Galliano
1/3 ounce orange curaçao
1/3 ounce half-and-half

Pour the Galliano, which is yellow, into a shot glass. Gently pour the orange curaçao over the back of a spoon, allowing it to run slowly down to layer on top of the Galliano. Then layer the half-and-half on top of the orange curaçao the same way.

Smiling Tiger

Makes 1 drink

1 ounce Blavod black vodka
½ ounce black Sambuca
½ ounce vanilla vodka
¼ ounce vanilla extract
Orange juice
Half-and-half

An ancient Asian limerick says, "Smiling young lady of Riga, once went for a ride on a tiger. They returned from the ride, with the lady inside, and the smile on the face of the tiger."

Pour the Blavod, black Sambuca, vanilla vodka, and vanilla extract into a tall glass to create the black layer. Fill glass with ice. Add orange juice until glass is three-quarters full. To make the white stripe, slowly fill the rest of the way with half-and-half.

Florida Sunset

Makes 1 drink

1½ ounces orange-flavored vodka
½ ounce grenadine
Orange juice
Orange wheel

Fill a tall glass with ice. Pour in the orange-flavored vodka and the grenadine. Pack the glass again with ice, then slowly fill the glass with orange juice. The result will be a red layer on the bottom mixing together with the orange layer. Garnish with the orange wheel.

Road Rage at the Traffic Light

Makes 1 drink

1 ounce crème de noya
1 ounce coconut rum
½ ounce melon liqueur
¼ ounce 151 rum
3 ounces pineapple juice
3 ounces orange juice

Crème de noya (also called noyeaux) is a red almond-flavored liqueur. It's not used very often in drink recipes, but when you are looking for a light liqueur to use as a float, it fits the bill perfectly.

Fill a tall glass with ice and pour in the coconut rum and crème de noya to create the red layer. Pack the glass again with ice, then slowly fill the glass with the orange juice and the pineapple juice (for the yellow layer). Gently top the drink with the melon liqueur and 151 rum (for the green).

Cigar Band

Makes 1 drink

½ ounce amaretto
½ ounce Irish cream liqueur
½ ounce cognac

Pour the amaretto into a shot glass. Gently pour the Irish cream liqueur over the back of a spoon to slowly layer it on top of the amaretto. Then layer the cognac on the Irish cream the same way.

Captain's Stripes

Makes 1 drink

¼ *ounce coffee liqueur*
¼ *ounce Galliano*
¼ *ounce Irish cream liqueur*
¼ *ounce Captain Morgan Spiced Rum*

Pour the coffee liqueur into a shot glass. Gently pour the Galliano over the back of a spoon to layer it slowly on top of the coffee liqueur. Repeat with the Irish cream liqueur and the Captain Morgan Spiced Rum.

• •

Astro Pop

Makes 1 drink

¼ *ounce grenadine*
¼ *ounce crème de banana*
¼ *ounce melon liqueur*
¼ *ounce vodka*

The Astro Pop, a lollipop shaped like a rocket, is the longest-lasting pop on the planet. Spangler Candy purchased the Astro Pop brand from Nellson Candies in Los Angeles, California, on July 1, 1987.

Pour the grenadine into a shot glass. Gently pour the crème de banana over the back of a spoon to slowly layer it on top of the grenadine. Repeat with the melon liqueur and then with the vodka.

Coral Snake Bite

Makes 1 drink

1/3 ounce coffee liqueur
1/3 ounce Galliano
1/3 ounce cherry brandy

If you are ever in doubt about whether the bite of a Coral Snake Bite is dangerous, just remember this rhyme: "Red on yellow, kill a fellow; red on black, friend to Jack."

Pour the coffee liqueur into a shot glass. Gently pour the Galliano over the back of a spoon to layer it slowly on top of the coffee liqueur. Then layer the cherry brandy over the Galliano the same way.

Somewhere over the Rainbow

Makes 1 drink

1 ounce melon liqueur
1 ounce strawberry-flavored vodka
3 ounces sweet-n-sour mix
3 ounces pineapple juice
1 ounce Parfait Amour
1 ounce Goldschlager (optional)

Pour the melon liqueur in a tall glass, then fill with ice. Pour the vodka, sweet-n-sour, and pineapple juice in a shaker tin of ice. Shake, then strain on top of the melon liqueur. Float the Parfait Amour on top. Serve a shot of Goldschlager on the side for the gold at the end of the rainbow. (Be sure to swirl the bottle around a little before you pour to guarantee some gold flakes get in the shot.)

Rhinestone Dallas Cowboy

Makes 1 drink

½ ounce Goldschlager
½ ounce blue curaçao

This beautiful shooter is a combination created in honor of Glen Campbell's 1975 number one hit song, "Rhinestone Cowboy," and the Dallas Cowboys' 1975 SuperBowl win. Quarterback Roger Staubach, a member of the Pro Football Hall of Fame, led the Cowboys.

Shake up the Goldschlager bottle so that the gold is mixed well, then pour the Goldschlager into a shot glass. Gently pour the blue curaçao over the back of a spoon to layer it slowly on top of the Goldschlager.

- -

Mexican Flag

The colors of the Mexican flag stand for hope and victory (green), the purity of ideals (white), and the blood shed by national heroes (red). The flag emblem is an eagle on top of a cactus devouring a serpent.

Makes 1 drink

1/3 ounce green
    crème de menthe
1/3 ounce sloe gin
1/3 ounce peppermint schnapps

Pour the green crème de menthe into a shot glass. Gently pour the peppermint schnapps over the back of a spoon to layer it slowly on top of the green crème de menthe. Then layer the sloe gin on top of the peppermint schnapps the same way.

Neapolitan Nipple

Makes 1 drink

1/3 ounce dark crème de cacao
1/3 ounce vanilla schnapps
1/3 ounce strawberry-flavored vodka
Drop of red food coloring
Whipped cream
Maraschino cherry

Pour the dark crème de cacao into a shot glass. Gently pour the vanilla schnapps on top of the crème de cacao. Stir the red food coloring into the strawberry-flavored vodka, then layer on top. Top it all off with whipped cream and a cherry.

Easter Egg

Makes 1 drink

¼ ounce raspberry liqueur
¼ ounce crème de banana
¼ ounce Parfait Amour
¼ ounce half-and-half

Pour the raspberry liqueur into a shot glass. Gently pour the crème de banana over the back of a spoon to layer it slowly on top of the raspberry liqueur. Then repeat with the Parfait Amour and half-and-half in the same way.

Cruella DeVille

Makes 1 drink

½ ounce coffee liqueur
½ ounce half-and-half
1 maraschino cherry

Pour the coffee liqueur into a shot glass. Gently pour the half-and-half over the back of a spoon to layer it slowly on top of the coffee liqueur. Garnish with a maraschino cherry.

• •

Barbershop Pole

Makes 1 drink

¼ ounce grenadine
¼ ounce white crème de cacao
¼ ounce cherry brandy
¼ ounce chocolate-flavored vodka
Big gumball or chocolate malted ball

Pour the grenadine into a tall, narrow shot glass. Gently pour the white crème de cacao over the back of a spoon to layer it slowly on top of the grenadine. Then layer the cherry brandy and vodka the same way. Balance the candy on top of the glass (like the ball on top of a barbershop pole).

Wicked Witch's Socks

Makes 1 drink

1/3 ounce coffee liqueur
1/3 ounce white crème de cacao
1/3 ounce Blavod black vodka

> Did you ever wonder why we wear masks and costumes on Halloween? The ancient Celts thought that witches roamed the countryside on the night of October 31. In order to frighten and confuse them, they wore masks and costumes while walking outside at night.

Pour the coffee liqueur into a shot glass. Gently pour the white crème de cacao over the back of a spoon to layer it slowly on top of the coffee liqueur. Then layer the black vodka on top of the white crème de cacao the same way.

Double-Stuffed Oreo

Makes 1 drink

1 ounce vodka
1 ounce coffee liqueur
Milk or half-and-half
1 Oreo cookie

Fill a tall glass with ice, then pour in the vodka and the coffee liqueur. Pack the glass again with ice, and slowly fill the glass with milk or half-and-half. You can substitute vanilla- or chocolate-flavored vodka. Float the Oreo cookie on top.

An Irish Green-Eyed Blonde

Makes 1 drink

1/3 ounce melon liqueur
1/3 ounce crème de banana
1/3 ounce Irish cream liqueur

Pour the melon liqueur into a shot glass. Gently pour the crème de banana over the back of a spoon to layer it slowly on top of the melon liqueur. Then layer the Irish cream liqueur on top of the crème de banana the same way.

Minty-Fresh Striped Toothpaste

Makes 1 drink

¼ ounce Irish cream liqueur
¼ ounce half-and-half
¼ ounce green
    crème de menthe
¼ ounce butterscotch schnapps

The secret of keeping stripes separate while filling a toothpaste tube is a special nozzle containing four smaller pipes. The white paste is pumped through the main nozzle, and the other colors pass through the four smaller ones within it, creating stripes.

Pour the butterscotch schnapps into a shot glass. Gently pour the green crème de menthe over the back of a spoon to layer it slowly down on top of the butterscotch schnapps. Layer the Irish cream liqueur and half-and-half the same way.

chapter 6

Flaming Libations from Hell

Bailey's Comet

Makes 1 drink

1½ ounces Bailey's Irish Cream
1/8 ounce 151 rum
Pinch of cinnamon

Pour the Bailey's Irish Cream into a shot glass. Slowly pour the 151 rum on top of the Bailey's Irish Cream, then light with a lighter. Sprinkle cinnamon over the flame—it will make tiny firework-type sparkles, creating the comet effect. When the flame dies, drink.

Hunka Hunka Burning Love

Makes 1 drink

2 scoops banana ice cream
Milk
Half a banana
1 ounce 151 rum
1 ounce hazelnut liqueur
½ ounce raspberry liqueur
1 ounce raspberry-flavored vodka or rum

Elvis trivia: Elvis's favorite food was fried peanut-butter-and-banana sandwiches, according to the woman who made countless hundreds of them for him toward the end of his life. Here's a fried frozen version with jelly on top.

Pour the raspberry-flavored vodka or rum, hazelnut liqueur, raspberry liqueur, and banana ice cream into a blender. Add the milk little by little to reach a smooth consistency. Pour into a tall glass and stick the banana straight up on top. Pour the 151 rum all over the banana, then light.

S'mores

Makes 1 drink

½ ounce dark crème de cacao
¼ ounce butterscotch schnapps
¼ ounce Irish cream liqueur
1/8 ounce 151 rum
Toothpick
1 miniature marshmallow

Pour the dark crème de cacao into a shot glass. Gently layer the butterscotch schnapps on top of the crème de cacao. Repeat the layering process with the Irish cream liqueur and the 151 rum. Light the rum, roast the marshmallow, and drink the shot after the fire has died down.

- -

Statue of Liberty

Makes 1 drink

1/3 ounce grenadine
1/3 ounce white crème de cacao
1/3 ounce blue curaçao
1/8 ounce 151 rum

Pour the grenadine into a shot glass. Gently layer the white crème de cacao on top of the grenadine, then repeat with the blue curaçao and rum. Light. Hold the burning red, white, and blue shot/torch high, like the Statue of Liberty. Sing the first few bars of "The Star-Spangled Banner," then drink.

Burning Busch

Makes 1 drink

1 bottle Busch beer
1 ounce Southern Comfort
1/8 ounce 151 rum

Pour the Busch beer into a beer glass. Pour the Southern Comfort into a shot glass, and carefully layer the 151 rum on top. Light the shot, and let it burn for a bit so most of the rum burns away. Drop the shot into the beer and chug.

- -

Tiki Torch

Makes 1 drink

1 ounce dark rum
1 ounce coconut rum
½ ounce grenadine
Pineapple juice
Orange juice
Sweet-n-sour mix
1 ounce 151 rum
Tall Tiki mug

Fill the Tiki mug with ice. Pour in the dark rum, coconut rum, and grenadine. Fill with equal parts of pineapple juice, orange juice, and sweet-n-sour mix, then stir. Top the drink with the 151 rum and light. You can replace the coconut rum with light rum if you don't like the taste of coconut.

Branded Buttery Nipple

Makes 1 drink

½ ounce Irish cream liqueur
1/8 ounce 151 rum
½ ounce butterscotch schnapps

In the cocktail world, a Buttery Nipple is a layered shot of butterscotch schnapps and Irish cream liqueur. This version adds flammable rum on top, therefore making it a Branded Buttery Nipple.

Pour the butterscotch schnapps into a shot glass. Gently pour the Irish cream liqueur over the back of a spoon to layer it slowly on top of the butterscotch schnapps. Then layer the 151 rum on top of the Irish cream the same way and light.

Wish upon a Burning Star

Makes 1 drink

1½ ounces Goldschlager
1/8 ounce 151 rum (divided into two equal parts)
Sugar
Cinnamon
Bamboo skewer
Star fruit slice

Mix a tablespoon of sugar with a pinch of cinnamon. Skewer the star fruit and dip into the mixture. Pour the shot of Goldschlager into a shot glass. Float one-half of the 151 rum on top of the Goldschlager and light. Pour the remaining rum over the skewered star fruit and hold over the flame to light. Make a wish, blow out the flames, drink the shot, and eat the star fruit.

Roman Candle

Makes 1 drink

1½ ounces Sambuca Romana

Sambuca Romana is the best-known producer of sambuca. This liqueur is derived from the elderberry bush, which grows all over the hills of Italy and has an anise or licorice flavor. Black Sambuca is infused with coffee.

Pour the Sambuca Romana into a shot glass, then light. Grab the lit shot, hold it straight up in the air, and say, "Hail Ceasar!" Blow it out, then drink. You can also use black Sambuca if that is available.

· ·

Fiery Sunset Tea

Makes 1 drink

½ ounce vodka
½ ounce gin
½ ounce rum
½ ounce tequila
½ ounce triple sec
Sweet-n-sour mix
1 ounce cranberry juice
½ ounce 151 rum

Pour the vodka, gin, rum, tequila, and triple sec into a tall glass of ice. Pack glass with ice, fill with sweet-n-sour mix, and stir. Top the drink with the cranberry juice, then with the 151 rum, and light. If you don't like tequila, just omit it from the recipe.

Dragon's Breath

Makes 1 drink

½ ounce green crème de menthe
½ ounce gold tequila
1/8 ounce Grand Marnier

Pour the green crème de menthe into a shot glass. Gently pour the gold tequila over the back of a spoon to layer it slowly on top of the green crème de menthe. Repeat with the Grand Marnier and light—you have a fiery dragon.

Sex in Front of the Fireplace

Makes 1 drink

1 ounce raspberry liqueur
1 ounce orange-
*   flavored vodka*
1 ounce peach schnapps
White cranberry juice
Orange juice
3 miniature Tootsie Rolls
½ ounce Grand Marnier
Long fireplace match

When making this drink, the raspberry liqueur should be at the bottom so when the orange layer is added, the layers resemble flames. The little Tootsie Rolls look like logs on the fire.

Pour the raspberry liqueur into a tall glass, then fill with ice. Pour in the vodka and peach schnapps and slowly fill with equal parts of white cranberry and orange juice. Garnish the top of the drink with the Tootsie Rolls (logs), pour the Grand Marnier on top, and light.

Hot Apple Pie

Makes 1 drink

¼ ounce Apple Pucker schnapps
¼ ounce cinnamon schnapps
¼ ounce Irish cream liqueur
¼ ounce Captain Morgan Spiced Rum
1/8 ounce 151 rum
Whipped cream

Pour the Apple Pucker schnapps, cinnamon schnapps, Irish cream liqueur, and Captain Morgan Spiced Rum into a shot glass. Carefully float the 151 rum on top and light. Put out the flame with a dollop of whipped cream. Eat the whipped cream, then drink the shot.

Blinded by the Light

Makes 1 drink

1 ounce light rum
Crystal Light Pink Lemonade
1/8 ounce 151 rum
Glow-light stick (thoroughly cleaned)
Flash paper

Flash paper can be purchased at your local magic shop. It's cool stuff! A small piece of it can create a very big and bright flame. After it lights, make sure to get your hands away quickly.

Pour the light rum into a tall glass of ice, then fill with the Crystal Light Pink Lemonade. Break the glow-light stick, and drop it in the drink. Top the drink with 151 rum and light. While the drink is flaming, hold the flash paper in your palms and light it with the flame.

Hawaiian Volcano

Makes 1 drink

2 ounces Passoa liqueur
1 ounce dark rum
5 ounces piña colada mix
1 ounce 151 rum

Pour the Passoa into a tall, clear glass. Pour the dark rum and piña colada mix into a blender with a cup of ice. Blend until smooth. Slowly pour into the glass and watch the Passoa rise like red lava up the glass. Top the drink with the 151 rum and light.

- -

Meteorite

Makes 1 drink

1 ounce sambuca (divided into two equal parts)
½ ounce coffee liqueur
Hot coffee
2 spoons of sugar
Lemon slice
Whipped cream

Rub lemon over the rim and the inside of a clear glass coffee mug, then coat with sugar. Pour half of the sambuca into the glass and light to caramelize the sugar. This is the meteorite entering the atmosphere. Carefully pour in the rest of the sambuca and the coffee liqueur. Fill with coffee and garnish with whipped cream.

Sacrifice to the Gods

Makes 1 drink

1½ ounces dark crème de cacao
Milk or half-and-half
1½ ounces brandy
Pinch of nutmeg

Half-fill a tall glass with ice and add the dark crème de cacao. Fill with milk or half-and-half (depending on your dietary needs), then sprinkle the nutmeg on top. Pour the brandy into a shot glass, light, and pour the shot into the drink to make your sacrifice.

Eternal Flame

Makes 1 drink

Reese's Peanut Butter Cup
½ ounce Dooley's toffee liqueur
½ ounce coffee liqueur
3/4 ounce Grand Marnier
        (divided inuo two parts: ½ ounce and ¼ ounce)

Reese's Peanut Butter Cups are the best-selling candy in the United States. Reese's makes enough peanut butter cups in one year to feed one cup to every person in the United States, Japan, Europe, Australia, China, Africa, and India.

Pour the toffee liqueur, coffee liqueur, and the ½ ounce of Grand Marnier into a shot glass. Cut a small hole in the middle of the Reese's Peanut Butter Cup. Set it on top of the shot glass, pour in the remaining ¼ ounce of Grand Marnier, and light. When the flame dies, drink and then eat the candy.

Hot-Blooded

Makes 1 drink

1½ ounces tequila
Tabasco sauce
1/8 ounce 151 rum

Tabasco, the popular Louisiana hot sauce, comes from Avery Island, which is 140 miles west of New Orleans. It has been produced since 1868. Each 2-ounce Tabasco bottle sauce contains about 720 drops of sauce.

Pour the tequila into a shot glass and add several dashes of Tabasco. Gently layer the 151 rum on top, then light. Let the flame die all the way down to burn off all the rum. Drink. You can replace the 151 rum with Grand Marnier or sambuca if you prefer.

Ring of Fire

Makes 1 drink

½ ounce Frangelico
½ ounce Irish cream liqueur
Hot coffee
½ ounce Grand Marnier
Glazed donut

Pour the Frangelico, Irish cream liqueur, and hot coffee into an Irish coffee mug. Set the glazed donut on the rim of the mug and pour the Grand Marnier over it. Light the donut to get your ring of fire. When the flame has died, have your coffee and doughnut.

chapter 7

Happily-Ever-After Dinner Drinks

Snow White Caramel Apple Cider

Makes 1 drink

1 ounce Dooley's toffee liqueur
½ ounce Tuaca
Hot apple cider
Whipped cream (optional)

The original recipe for Tuaca dates to the Renaissance. It is still crafted today as it always has been, by the Tuoni family in Livorno, Italy. The taste is light, smooth vanilla with just a tiny hint of citrus.

Pour the Dooley's toffee liqueur and Tuaca into a coffee mug and fill with hot apple cider. Top with whipped cream if you desire. If you don't like the taste of Tuaca, you can replace it with an equal amount of Dooley's or applejack brandy.

Gretel's Hot Gingerbread Toddy

Makes 1 drink

½ cup water
1-inch knob of fresh ginger, thinly sliced
1/8 cup sugar
1 ounce rum
1 cup hot apple cider

Combine the water and ginger in a saucepan and bring to a boil. Remove from heat, cover, and let steep 30 minutes. Add the sugar and bring to a boil again, stirring until the sugar dissolves (about 3 minutes). Strain ¼ cup into a mug and add the rum. Fill with hot apple cider.

Sugar and Spice and Everything Nice

Makes 1 drink

Bottle or can of Guinness stout
¼ cup sweetened condensed milk
Pinch of cinnamon
Pinch of nutmeg
1 packet hot cocoa mix

Chill the Guinness and the condensed milk (unless you prefer your drinks at room temperature, European style). Pour the
Guinness into a bowl. Add the condensed milk, cinnamon, nutmeg, and cocoa mix, then stir until blended. Pour into a tall beer
glass and enjoy.

- -

Goldilocks Platinum-Blonde Coffee

Makes 1 drink

1½ ounces Godiva white chocolate liqueur
Black coffee
Whipped cream (optional)

Pour the Godiva white chocolate liqueur into a coffee mug and fill
with coffee. Garnish with whipped cream if desired. You can substitute Godet or Mozart white chocolate liqueurs for the Godiva.
You can also add a little half-and-half to this recipe to lighten it
up a bit more.

Papa Bear's Black Honey

Makes 1 drink

1½ ounces Drambuie
Honey
Coffee
Whipped cream (optional)

Drambuie is a Scottish liqueur made from aged Scotch whiskey, heather honey, and other, secret ingredients. The word Drambuie in Gaelic means "the drink that satisfies." It has been in production since 1745.

Pour the Drambuie into a mug and fill with coffee. Stir a spoonful of honey (to taste) into the drink. Top with whipped cream if you desire. If the drink is sweet enough with just the Drambuie, then omit the honey.

Grandma's Southern Blackberry Cobbler

Makes 1 drink

1½ ounces blackberry brandy
½ ounce Southern Comfort

Pour the blackberry brandy and Southern Comfort into a short glass of ice and stir. This is a simple cocktail to make and a flavorful one to sip. Without any mixers, it does taste a little potent. Apricot brandy can be substituted for the blackberry.

Jiminy Cricket Grasshopper

Makes 1 drink

1 ounce green crème de menthe
1 ounce white crème de cacao
2 ounces half-and-half
Grated chocolate

Pour the green crème de menthe, white crème de cacao, and half-and-half into a shaker tin of ice. Shake, then strain into a martini glass and garnish with grated chocolate. This drink can also be served over ice or blended. If you add an ounce of vodka, you can make it a Flying Grasshopper.

· ·

Pocahontas Nuts and Berries

Makes 1 drink

1 ounce Frangelico
1 ounce Chambord
Half-and-half or milk

The nuts-and-berries flavor in this cocktail comes from the Frangelico and Chambord. Frangelico is a hazelnut liqueur, and Chambord is a black raspberry liqueur. Both are low in alcohol. You can add vodka to make the drink stronger. Try raspberry vodka.

Pour the Frangelico and Chambord into a short glass of ice, then fill with half-and-half or milk. You can also make this drink straight up by pouring the Frangelico, Chambord, and three ounces of half-and-half into a shaker tin of ice. Shake, then strain into a martini glass.

Black Mother Goose

Makes 1 drink

1 ounce Grey Goose vodka
1 ounce coffee liqueur

Pour the Grey Goose vodka and coffee liqueur into a short glass of ice and stir. You can also add half-and-half or milk to the recipe. Mixing vodka and coffee liqueur together makes a Black Russian. If you add half-and-half, it's called a White Russian.

- -

Jack Be Nimble Java

Makes 1 drink

½ ounce Jack Daniel's
1 ounce amaretto
Coffee
Whipped cream (optional)

Jack Daniel's is a sour mash whiskey made in Lynchburg, Tennessee. It gets its flavor from being filtered through ten feet of sugar maple charcoal before aging in American white oak barrels.

Pour the Jack Daniel's and amaretto into a mug and fill with coffee. If you desire, top with whipped cream. You could also add a dash of amaretto-flavored creamer. If you prefer your drink a little stronger, switch the amounts of the Jack Daniel's and amaretto.

Alice in Wonderland Green Mint Tea

Makes 1 drink

5 mint leaves
2 spoonfuls simple syrup (page 111)
2 lime slices
1 ounce light rum
Hot green tea
Honey

In a mug, muddle the mint in the simple syrup with the lime slices. Add the light rum, then pour steaming green tea on top. Sweeten with honey to taste. You can make the mint/lime syrup ahead of time and can even make extra if you wish. Strained loose green tea or a tea bag can be used.

. . . .

Dorothy's Ruby Sipper

Makes 1 drink

1½ ounces Dekuyper Hot Damn Cinnamon Schnapps
Hot apple cider

Pour the cinnamon schnapps into a coffee mug, then fill with hot apple cider. Other brands of cinnamon schnapps also work with this recipe, but the Dekuyper schnapps is colored red and looks more like a traditional cinnamon candy. Why not drop in a few red-hots as well?

The Frog Prince in a Blender

Makes 1 drink

1½ ounces coffee liqueur
½ ounce green crème de menthe
½ ounce Dekuyper Hot Damn Cinnamon Schnapps

Pour the coffee liqueur, green crème de menthe, and Hot Damn Cinnamon Schnapps into a blender with a cup of ice. Blend until smooth to make your Frog Prince in a Blender, then pour into a glass of your choice. You can also serve this drink straight up. Just shake it in a shaker tin of ice and strain into a martini glass.

Sleeping Beauty's Butterscotch Coffee

Makes 1 drink

1 ounce butterscotch schnapps
½ ounce Frangelico
Coffee
½ ounce hazelnut
    creamer (optional)

Have you ever wondered what gives butterscotch its flavor? Basically, it comes from butter, brown sugar, and vanilla. Reed's came out with the very first candy in 1931. Jell-O brand followed in 1932 by marketing butterscotch pudding.

Pour the butterscotch schnapps and the Frangelico into a coffee mug and fill with coffee. For a nice creamy touch, add the hazelnut creamer and stir. If you don't like the subtle nutty flavor, then omit the Frangelico and hazelnut creamer and add another half ounce of butterscotch schnapps instead.

Fairy Godmother

Makes 1 drink

1½ ounces amaretto
1½ ounces vodka

Pour the amaretto and vodka into a short glass of ice and stir. This recipe is for a traditional Fairy Godmother. If you prefer a Fairy Godfather instead, replace the vodka with Scotch whiskey. This drink can also be served straight up. Just shake it in a shaker tin of ice and strain into a martini glass.

Rimmed Brothers Grimm Cocoa

Makes 1 drink

1 ounce Kirschwasser
1 packet hot cocoa
Hot water
1 spoonful grenadine
1 spoonful sugar
Pinch of cinnamon
Whipped cream or miniature marshmallows (optional, for garnish)

Mix the sugar and cinnamon together on a saucer. Dip the rim of a mug into the grenadine, then into the cinnamon sugar. Pour the Kirschwasser and the packet of cocoa into the mug. Fill with hot water and stir. Garnish with whipped cream or miniature marshmallows if desired.

Hot Buttered Sugarplum Rum

Makes 1 drink

1 ounce dark rum
½ ounce plum liqueur
2 spoonfuls
    hot buttered-rum mix
Hot water

Plums originate from Damascus, Syria, and from Persia. They have stones that, like human fingerprints, are each one unique. The most popular food item made with plums is plum sauce, which is also called Chinese duck sauce.

Pour the dark rum, plum liqueur, and hot buttered-rum mix into a mug. Fill with hot water and stir to dissolve. You can substitute light rum if desired or omit the rum altogether. Try this recipe with homemade Hot Buttered Rum Mix (page 118).

Magic Wand Espresso

Makes 1 drink

1½ ounces sambuca
Cup of espresso
Star fruit slice
Bamboo skewer
2 heaping spoons of confectioner's sugar

Moisten the star fruit slice in water. Dip in the sugar and skewer. Pour the sambuca into an espresso cup and fill with espresso. Tap the magic wand on the rim to sprinkle the drink with sugar.

The Queen Bee Stinger

Makes 1 drink

2 ounces Crown Royal Canadian whiskey
1 ounce white crème de menthe

Pour the Crown Royal and the white crème de menthe into an attractive short glass filled with ice and stir. A traditional cocktail called a Stinger is made with brandy or cognac and white crème de menthe. This recipe is a new version of that classic. You can substitute another whiskey for the Crown.

- -

Golden Eggnog Grog

Makes 1 drink

1½ ounces dark rum
Eggnog
Pinch of nutmeg

It is believed that "Old Grog" was the nickname of eccentric admiral Edward Vernon from the eighteenth century. Rather than wine, he kept rum on his ships, which eventually gained the nickname "grog."

Pour the dark rum into a glass of your choice and fill with eggnog. If the eggnog is cold, you don't need to add ice. Garnish with a pinch of nutmeg. You can substitute light rum, brandy, cognac, or whiskey for the dark rum.

chapter 8

Lustful Liquid Aphrodisiacs

Liquid Viagra

Makes 1 drink

1 ounce vodka
½ ounce blue curaçao
½ ounce apricot brandy
½ ounce lime juice

Pour all the ingredients over ice in a short glass to sip this as a drink. Or pour all the ingredients into a shaker tin of ice, shake, and strain into a glass of your choice to enjoy as a shooter.

Habla Español Fly

Makes 1 drink

1½ ounces tequila
1½ ounces coffee liqueur
5 ounces chilled black coffee
1 ounce half-and-half

The real Spanish fly is a highly toxic ground insect from South America that, if you were to ever encounter, you would not want to ingest. It is highly poisonous when swallowed and can also be absorbed through the skin.

Pour all the ingredients into a tall glass of ice and stir. It will be like an iced coffee. You can also add more coffee and half-and-half, to taste, or reduce the coffee and half-and-half to make a shooter.

Pear Phero Moan

Makes 1 drink

1 ounce pear schnapps
½ ounce pear nectar
Dry champagne
Strawberry (for garnish)

Pour the pear schnapps and pear nectar into a tall fluted champagne glass. Fill with very dry (brut) champagne. Garnish the rim with a strawberry. For even more of a kick, substitute some or all of the pear schnapps with vodka—plain or vanilla.

- -

Berry Bordello

Makes 1 drink

1 ounce strawberry vodka
½ ounce raspberry vodka
½ ounce raspberry liqueur
Cranberry juice
Berries for garnish

Pour the first three ingredients into a tall glass of ice. Fill with cranberry juice and stir. (If you prefer a fizzy drink, fill the glass half with cranberry juice and half with 7-Up.) Garnish with your choice of berries, like a handful of blueberries or raspberries, or a strawberry on the rim.

Mai Tai Me Up

Makes 1 drink

1 ounce dark rum
½ ounce light rum
½ ounce 151 rum
1½ ounces pineapple juice
1½ ounces sweet-n-sour mix
1 slice canned pineapple
Maraschino cherry

The Mai Tai became popular at Trader Vic's restaurants in Oakland, San Francisco, and Seattle. In 1953, Vic introduced the Mai Tai to Hawaii at the Royal Hawaiian Hotels. There have been many variations on the recipe.

Pour all the liquid ingredients into a shaker tin of ice. Shake, then strain into a glass of your choice. You can make this in an over-sized glass by adding more sweet-n-sour. Garnish with the pineapple, and drop the cherry into the pineapple hole.

Blue Taboo

Makes 1 drink

1 ounce blueberry schnapps
½ ounce blue curaçao
½ ounce vodka
Sweet-n-sour mix
7-Up
Maraschino cherry

Pour the first three ingredients into a tall glass of ice. Fill with equal amounts of sweet-n-sour mix and 7-Up. Garnish with the maraschino cherry.

Who's Your Daddy?

Makes 1 drink

1 ounce Dooley's toffee liqueur
½ ounce Tuaca
½ ounce vanilla vodka
1 large scoop vanilla ice cream
Half-and-half or milk
Sugar Daddy caramel sucker

Put the first four ingredients into a blender. Add about an ounce of milk or half-and-half to help the blending process. Keep adding milk or half-and-half and ice cubes little by little to achieve a thick but drinkable consistency. Pour into a tall glass, and stick the Sugar Daddy on top.

* * *

In the Mood

Makes 1 drink

1 ounce dark crème de cacao
1 ounce dark rum
3 ounces half-and-half
*   or milk*
1 spoonful hot cocoa mix

There are other chocolate-flavored liquors and liqueurs on the market that you can try in this cocktail. Try replacing the dark crème de cacao with light crème de cacao or Kahlua, and substitute chocolate vodka for the dark rum.

Moisten the rim of a martini glass with water and dip in the hot cocoa mix. Pour the first three ingredients into a shaker tin of ice. Shake and strain into the glass. You can also serve this drink on the rocks in a tall glass—just add more half-and-half.

Rummy Moulin Rouge

Makes 1 drink

½ ounce light rum
½ ounce dark rum
½ ounce 151 rum
½ ounce coconut rum
½ ounce spiced rum

½ ounce grenadine
Pineapple juice
Pineapple and
    maraschino cherry

Pour the first six ingredients into a tall glass packed with ice. Fill glass with pineapple juice and stir. Garnish with a slice of pineapple and a maraschino cherry. If there is a rum that you don't care for, then just omit it and add the same amount of another that you do like.

· ·

Barely Legal

Makes 1 drink

1 ounce amaretto
1 ounce 151 rum
Dr Pepper

Try serving this cocktail with the Spicy Almond Dip (page 175), the Stuffed Sweet Peppers (page 200), or the Wild Almond Apple Rice (page 228).

Pour the amaretto and 151 rum into a tall glass of ice. Fill with Dr Pepper and stir. You can substitute regular rum for the "barely legal" 151 rum, if you wish, and Mr. Pibb makes a fine substitute for Dr Pepper. Do not omit the amaretto—it is an essential ingredient.

Love Potion #9

Makes 1 drink

1 ounce Parfait Amour
1 ounce mandarin vodka
White cranberry juice
Sprig of purple seedless grapes

This is an excellent cocktail to make at a Valentine's party for two or for twenty-two. It's also a great drink for a girls' night in.

Pour the Parfait Amour and mandarin vodka into a tall glass of ice and fill with white cranberry juice. Break off a sprig of purple seedless grapes and garnish the top of the drink. You can use green seedless grapes as well. Either color will complement the purple color of the drink.

Afternoon Delight

Makes 1 drink

I ounce banana vodka or rum
1 ounce banana liqueur
1 ounce white crème de cacao
1 scoop of banana ice cream
1 scoop of chocolate ice cream

Pour all the ingredients into a blender. Blend until smooth. If you prefer a creamier drink, add half-and-half or milk little by little while the blender is on. The goal is to reach a thick but drink-able consistency. If you cannot find banana ice cream, you can substitute vanilla.

Melonlicious Mistress

Makes 1 drink

1 ounce Midori
1 ounce lemon-flavored vodka or rum
7-Up
Maraschino cherry

Pour the Midori and lemon-flavored vodka or rum into a tall glass of ice. Fill with 7-Up and stir. Garnish with a maraschino cherry. For a tasty drink with less alcohol, omit the vodka or rum. You can also substitute diet 7-Up to cut down the calories.

Come Hither

Makes 1 drink

1 ounce vanilla vodka
1 ounce white crème de cacao
½ ounce Galliano
2 ounces half-and-half

Pour the vanilla vodka, white crème de cacao, Galliano, and half-and-half into a shaker tin of ice. Shake, then strain into a glass of your choice. You can substitute dark crème de cacao for the white; however, the drink will turn a light brown. Add more half-and-half to taste if desired.

Charming Proposal

Makes 1 drink

½ ounce Passoa
¼ ounce grenadine
Ginger ale
½ ounce lemon-flavored rum
½ ounce sour apple schnapps

Passoa is a liqueur made from passion fruit juice. Make sure that you don't omit this from the recipe, because it is an essential ingredient.

Pour the first four ingredients into a tall glass of ice and stir. Fill the rest of the way with ginger ale and stir again.

• •

Coconut Concubine

Makes 1 drink

1 ounce coconut rum
1 ounce vanilla vodka
1 ounce Coco Lopez
Pineapple juice
Orange juice
Grenadine
Pineapple and maraschino cherry

Pour the coconut rum, vanilla vodka, and Coco Lopez into a tall glass of ice. Fill with equal amounts of pineapple and orange juice. Splash in the grenadine, then stir. Garnish with a pineapple slice and cherry. You can also make this drink in the blender. Simply measure the contents into the glass first, then pour the contents into the blender.

Spiced Forbidden Fruit

Makes 1 drink

1 ounce spiced rum
1 ounce apple schnapps
¼ ounce cinnamon schnapps
7-Up

Everyone knows that the forbidden fruit was an apple that grew in the Garden of Eden on the Tree of Knowledge of Good and Evil, which was off-limits to Adam and Eve. Well, here's a liquid apple to sample—minus the snake.

Pour the spiced rum, apple schnapps, and cinnamon schnapps into a tall glass of ice. Fill with 7-Up. It's important to mix this drink well. Pour the contents into an empty glass, then back again to achieve a good mix. If you don't like cinnamon, then omit it from the recipe.

Black Magic

Makes 1 drink

2 ounces Blavod black vodka
½ ounce grenadine
7-Up
Maraschino cherry

Pour the Blavod and grenadine into a tall glass of ice. Fill with 7-Up and stir. Garnish with a maraschino cherry. This drink is a mystical blackish-gray color and tastes like an adult version of a Shirley Temple. Reduce the amount of vodka for less of an impact.

Strawberry Sexual Healing

Makes 1 drink

6 fresh strawberries
Small handful of fresh mint leaves
Juice from half a lime
1 ounce water
1 spoon sugar
1½ ounces light rum
Cheesecloth or fine-mesh strainer

Stem the strawberries. Put all the ingredients except the rum into a shaker tin and mash together. Add a scoop of ice and the rum. Shake long and hard. Place the cheesecloth or strainer over a glass of your choice and strain.

- -

Lemon Love Shack Shake

Makes 1 drink

1 ounce Cointreau
2 ounces half-and-half
1 big scoop Italian lemon ice
1 ounce lemon-flavored vodka

This creamy lemon-flavored libation goes great with seafood. Try the South-of-the-Border Shrimp Cocktail (page 208), Shrimp Artichoke Spirals (page 234), or the Cajun Shrimp Kabobs (page 261).

Put all the ingredients into a blender. Blend until smooth. Add more Italian lemon ice for more of a lemony taste. To make it creamier, add more half-and-half. You might have to add some ices cubes as well. To save some money, you can replace the Cointreau with triple sec or another orange liqueur.

chapter 9

Holiday, Seasonal, and Party Mixes

Sparkling New Year Cheer

Makes 1 drink

1 sugar cube
6 dashes Angostura bitters
Chilled champagne
Strip of lemon rind

Dash a sugar cube with Angostura bitters and drop into the bottom of a champagne flute. Fill with champagne. Twist the strip of lemon rind to release the oils. Rub around the rim of the glass and drop into the drink.

- -

Super Bowl Drop Kick

Makes 1 drink

1 can or bottle beer
1 ounce American whiskey

Fill a beer glass with beer, then pour an American whiskey into a shot glass. Here's where the drop kick comes in: Drop the shot into the beer, then kick the whole thing (beer and all) down your throat in one fell swoop.

Kama Sutra

Makes 1 drink

½ ounce Passoa
½ ounce Alize Red Passion
½ ounce Cheri-berri Pucker
Sprite
Maraschino cherries

This is a very erotic Valentine cocktail filled with lots of passion and pucker! You can also shake the alcohol in a shaker tin of ice, omitting the Sprite, then strain into a martini glass.

Pour the Passoa, Alize Red Passion, and Cheri-berri Pucker into a tall glass, then add ice. Fill to the top with Sprite and garnish with maraschino cherries. When you make the drink this way, it will look layered. Add vodka if you'd like to bump it up a notch.

- -

Ragin' Cajun Mardi Gras Punch

Makes 20 drinks

1 bottle (750 ml) of chilled citrus-flavored vodka
2 40-ounce bottles of chilled grape juice
2 48-ounce cans of chilled pineapple juice
1 2-liter bottle of chilled ginger ale
A bunch of green seedless grapes
Fishing line and a needle

Make an ice ring: Fill half a ring mold with 1 bottle of grape juice, freeze, fill with 1 can of pineapple juice, and freeze again. String the grapes on the fishing line to make beads. Pour the vodka, remaining grape and pineapple juice, and ginger ale into a punch bowl. Place the ice ring and the string of grapes in the bowl.

Irish Car Bomb

Makes 1 drink

1 pint of Guinness stout
½ ounce Irish whiskey
½ ounce Baileys Irish Cream

Pour the Guinness into a pint glass. Pour in the Irish whiskey into a shot glass, then gently pour the Baileys over the back of a spoon to layer it slowly on top. Drop the shot into the beer, then drink.

April Fool's Mind Eraser

Makes 2 drinks

2 ounces coffee liqueur
2 ounces vodka
Sprite or club soda
2 straws

Use a pin to make a hole in one of the straws. The whole joke is that your friend, the April Fool, won't be able to suck down his or her drink as quickly as you.

Prep one of the straws by poking a hole in it. Fill two short glasses with ice. Pour one ounce of coffee liqueur and one ounce of vodka into each. Fill both with Sprite or club soda. Stick in the straws, and suck down as fast as you can.

White Chocolate Easter Bunny

Makes 1 drink

½ ounce vanilla vodka
1 ounce white chocolate liqueur
2 ounces eggnog
1 ounce half-and-half
Jelly beans

Pour the vanilla vodka, white chocolate liqueur, eggnog, and half-and-half into a shaker tin of ice. Shake, then strain into a martini glass. Hide your little Easter eggs by dropping some jelly beans into the glass to sink to the bottom. And so begins your white chocolate Easter Egg Hunt.

Wine-Tasting Mama

Makes multiple drinks

Several bottles of wine (all different)
2 pitchers of water
Lots of wine glasses

This is an inexpensive way to celebrate Mother's Day. Have all the guests bring the bottle of wine of their choice to your wine-tasting party. After collecting the wine, line up all the bottles in a designated area, uncork them, and allow guests to sample all the wines. Set out water pitchers.

Bachelorette Strip, Skip, and Go Naked

Makes 1 drink

2 ounces lime-flavored gin

5 ounces limeade

½ ounce grenadine

Beer

Lime or a cherry

Having a keg at your party? This recipe is great for the girls. They can make their drink with the gin, limeade, and grenadine, then walk over to the keg and top it off.

Pour the lime-flavored gin, limeade, and grenadine into a tall glass of ice, then fill with beer. Garnish with a lime or a cherry. You can find limeade in your grocer's freezer next to the frozen orange juice. The grenadine adds a little bit of sweetness as well as a girly color.

Thank God I'm Finally Twenty-One!

Makes 1 drink

½ ounce coffee liqueur

½ ounce Irish cream liqueur

Squirt of whipped cream

Pour the coffee liqueur into a shot glass, then gently pour the Irish cream liqueur on top. Top with whipped cream. Put your hands behind your back, suck out the whipped cream, wrap your lips around the shot glass, tilt it back and swallow, then put the shot glass back down with your mouth.

Wedding Reception Bubbles

Makes 1 drink

½ ounce strawberry-flavored vodka
1 ounce strawberry liqueur
Dry champagne
1 strawberry

Pour the strawberry vodka and the strawberry liqueur into a champagne flute, then fill with champagne. Garnish the rim with a strawberry. The reason it's best to use dry (rather than sweet) champagne is because the liqueur will sweeten it enough. Just look for the words "Dry" or "Brut" on the label.

. . . .

Sensational Summertime Slushies

Makes 25 drinks

1 bottle (750 ml) vanilla vodka
1 bottle (750 ml) coconut rum
1 gallon orange juice
1 gallon pineapple juice
2 2-liter bottles of citrus soda

This is a great slushy summertime drink to make up ahead of time and keep in the freezer. It's perfect for a family BBQ or when unexpected guests show up on a hot day. Besides that, it is just so yummy!

Pour the vanilla vodka, coconut rum, orange juice, and pineapple juice into a big bowl or pot. Stir. Set in the freezer for at least twenty-four hours or until frozen. When frozen, place two scoops in a tall glass, then fill with the citrus soda. You can substitute Fresca for the citrus soda.

Hawaiian Luau Jungle Juice

Makes 30–40 drinks

2 bottles (750 ml) dark rum
2 bottles (750 ml) light rum
1 gallon orange juice
1 gallon pineapple juice
1 gallon sweet-n-sour mix
1 bottle grenadine
5-gallon Igloo water cooler
Brown mailing paper
Black magic marker
Bag of ice
Jar of maraschino cherries
Lots of pineapple slices
Box of paper parasols

This recipe is for a luau. The idea is to make it self-service. Set cups and all the garnishes around it. Make sure you set it up in an open area for crowd control.

Pour the dark rum, light rum, orange and pineapple juice, sweet-n-sour mix, and grenadine into the water cooler. Add the bag of ice and stir. Draw Tiki totem-pole designs on the brown paper, then wrap around the cooler. Cut a hole for the spigot. Set the cherries, pineapple slices, and parasols out around this self-service oasis.

Born on the 4th of July

Makes 1 drink

1½ ounces cherry-flavored vodka or rum
½ ounce blue curaçao
3 ounces white cranberry juice
1 maraschino cherry

Pour the cherry-flavored vodka or rum and the white cranberry juice into a shaker tin of ice. Shake, then strain into a martini glass. Drop the cherry in, then carefully float the blue curaçao on top by pouring it over the back of a spoon.

Autumn in New York

Makes 1 drink

1 ounce applejack brandy
½ ounce Tuaca
Hot apple cider
Whipped cream (optional)

Pour the applejack brandy and Tuaca into a mug, then fill with hot apple cider. Top with whipped cream from a can, if you desire. You can play around with this recipe by exchanging the amounts of the applejack brandy and Tuaca. Or you can eliminate one and double the other.

You Don't Know Jack o'Lantern Punch

Makes multiple drinks

Half bottle (750 ml) of chilled Jack Daniel's
Quarter of a bottle (750 ml) of chilled triple sec
Chilled lemonade
Chilled Sprite
1 large pumpkin
Round glass bowl
Glow sticks (thoroughly cleaned)

Hollow out and carve the pumpkin. Insert a round clear bowl inside, then place in the freezer overnight to chill. When ready to serve, pour the Jack Daniel's, triple sec, lemonade, and Sprite into the bowl and stir. Add the glow sticks and ladle over ice to serve. Place in a dark area for the best effect.

Thanksgiving Turkey Cosmo

Makes 1 drink

1½ ounces Wild Turkey
½ ounce triple sec
¼ ounce lime juice
2 ounces cranberry juice

There's no better cocktail for Thanksgiving than this one. Your guests will find it amusing. Keep a smile on their faces by serving them Thanksgiving Turkey Casserole in a Pumpkin (page 255).

Pour all ingredients into a shaker tin of ice. Shake, then strain into a martini glass. If you don't have a bottle of triple sec around and want to save some money, simply omit it from the recipe. The other ingredients are essential.

Snowball Fight

Makes 1 drink

1½ ounces vanilla vodka
½ teaspoon vanilla extract
2 spoons sugar or Splenda
Half-and-half or milk
Crushed ice
Sprinkle of cinnamon for garnish

Fill a tall glass with crushed ice. Add the vanilla vodka, vanilla extract, sugar or Splenda, and fill with half-and-half or milk. Add more sugar or Splenda to taste, then garnish with a sprinkle of cinnamon. You can use plain vodka if you like, but the vanilla really makes a difference.

Holly Berry

Makes 1 drink

1½ ounces raspberry vodka
½ ounce triple sec
¼ ounce Roses lime juice
3 ounces cranberry juice
Washed holly sprig with berries (optional)

Pour the raspberry vodka, triple sec, Roses lime juice, and cranberry juice into a shaker tin of ice. Shake, then strain into a martini glass. Garnish with a clean holly sprig with berries for a festive touch. (Don't eat the berries, which are toxic. Use a plastic replica if you wish.)

chapter 10

Homemade Creations

Flavored/Infused Vodka, Gin, and Rum

Makes 1 bottle

1 bottle (750 ml) vodka, gin, or rum
Fruit, spice, or herb of your choice

Find a large-mouthed glass container, such as a Mason jar, to make your infusions. Fresh fruit and produce should be washed well to remove all possible pesticides. Place your chosen fruit, spice, or herb in the container, add the vodka, gin, or rum (saving the bottle), and close the lid tightly. Keep out of direct sunlight and let sit from four days to two weeks (according to the following chart). Strain, and put back into the bottle when finished.

Food	Length of Time to Infuse
Vanilla beans, lemons, oranges, grapefruit, limes, mint, garlic, tarragon, basil, oregano, dill, thyme	4 days
Cantaloupes, strawberries, peaches, mangoes, pitted cherries, raspberries, blueberries, blackberries	1 week
Whole chili peppers, pineapple, fresh ginger, lemongrass	2 weeks

Raspberry Liqueur

Makes 2½ cups

1 pint fresh raspberries
2½ cups vodka
1 vanilla bean
¼ teaspoon allspice (whole)
½ cup simple syrup (page 111)

Wash the raspberries and lightly crush to help release their flavor. Add the vodka (saving the bottle), vanilla bean, and allspice. Stir, and store in a large-mouthed jar in a cool dark place for three weeks. Strain mixture through a cheesecloth, squeezing out all the juice you can. Pour back into bottle, and add simple syrup to taste. Age another 3–5 weeks.

Limoncello

Makes 1 bottle

1 bottle (750 ml) vodka
1 cup simple syrup (page 111)
Zest of 7 lemons

Wash lemons with a brush and hot water to remove any pesticides or wax, and zest the lemons. Pour half of the vodka into a gallon glass jar and add zest. Cover and let sit at room temperature for 20 days. Add the simple syrup and remaining vodka (saving the bottle) and let sit for another 20 days. Strain and discard the lemon zest, then put back into the bottle. Keep this one in the freezer until ready to serve. As a nice touch, serve in chilled cordial glasses.

Irish Cream

Makes 1 bottle

3/4 cup Irish whiskey
1 cup whipping cream
4 eggs
2 tablespoons chocolate-flavored syrup
2 teaspoons instant coffee granules
1 teaspoon vanilla extract
1 14-ounce can Eagle Brand condensed milk

Combine all ingredients, then blend until smooth. Store in a tightly covered container in refrigerator. Irish cream can be served one day after making and will be good for one month. Always stir before serving. (Don't confuse whipping cream with whipped cream.)

Chocolate-flavored syrup is different from chocolate syrup. Look for chocolate-flavored syrup in coffee shops. The most popular brand name for flavored coffee syrups is Torani.

Coffee Liqueur

Makes 2 bottles

5 cups sugar
8 cups water
1 cup instant coffee
5 tablespoons vanilla extract
½ bottle (750 ml) vodka

Add the sugar to the water, and boil until sugar is completely dissolved. Remove from heat and cool to room temperature. Stir in the instant coffee, vanilla extract, and vodka. Pour the mixture into a bottle or other glass container with a tight lid, and let it sit undisturbed in a cool, dark place for at least a month.

Simple Syrup

Makes 2 cups

2 cups sugar

2 cups water

To make a quick, no-cook simple syrup, simply fill a bottle half with sugar and half with water. Shake. After the cloudiness clears, shake again. For sugar-free simple syrup, replace sugar with Splenda.

Combine the sugar and the water in a pan. Heat until boiling, stirring constantly. Reduce heat to a bare simmer and continue to stir for another 5 minutes. Remove from heat and allow to cool. The result is simple syrup. This keeps in the refrigerator for a very long time.

Sweet-n-Sour/Margarita Mix

Makes 6 cups

Juice from 6 lemons

Juice from 6 limes

4 cups sugar

6 cups water

Sweet-n-sour mix is probably the most confusing mixer of all. Basically, it is a sweetened lemon/lime-flavored mix. It has many names: sweet-n-sour, margarita mix, whiskey sour mix, or just plain sour mix.

The way you make your sweet-n-sour mix depends on your personal preferences. Some people like it sweet, and others sour. When you mix the juice and simple syrup together, you are trying to reach a perfect balance of sweet with sour. Keep taste-testing until you find your preference. Splenda can be substituted.

Bloody Mary Mix

Makes 16 cups

2 (46-ounce) cans tomato juice
1 teaspoon celery salt
4 ounces lemon juice

1 (5-ounce) bottle
  Lea & Perrins
  Worcestershire sauce
Tabasco sauce to taste
Salt to taste

Mix all ingredients together and refrigerate. You can add all kinds of things to a basic Bloody Mary mix. Jazz it up by adding any of these: raw horseradish, lime juice, A-1 steak sauce, beef bouillon, wasabi, chili powder, bitters, or V-8 instead of regular tomato juice. Garnishes for a Bloody Mary include celery, scallion, lime, lemon, green olive, pickled pepperoncini pepper, peeled cocktail shrimp, cherry tomatoes, pickled okra, and pickled asparagus.

White Sangria

Serves 4

1 cup water
½ cup sugar
6 cinnamon sticks
1 bottle sweet white wine (not dry)
1 cup sparkling water

1 cup apple juice
½ cup orange juice
3 oranges cut in wheels
Lots of cherries
3 apples cut in chunks

Heat the water, sugar, and cinnamon sticks to a simmer. Continue to simmer for 5 minutes, and remove from heat. Let cool to room temperature. Remove the cinnamon sticks, and mix in all remaining liquid ingredients. Chill overnight in the refrigerator. Add the fruit when ready to serve for presentation.

Sangria

Serves 8

2 bottles red wine

2 tablespoons sugar

2 ounces brandy

1 cup orange juice

½ cup pineapple juice

½ cup cherry juice

3 cups maraschino cherries

1 orange, thinly sliced into wheels

1 lemon, thinly sliced into wheels

1 lime, thinly sliced into wheels

If you plan to present sangria in a bowl, freeze some of the mix in ice cube trays. Use the frozen cubes instead of ice so it doesn't get diluted.

Combine the first seven ingredients and half of the sliced fruit, and store in the refrigerator. When ready to serve, add the rest of the sliced fruit, reserving some for garnish. To make a non-alcoholic version, use nonalcoholic wine or grape juice. You are not limited to these fruits. All fruits are acceptable in sangria, so experiment.

Instant Cappuccino Mocha Mix

Serves 25

6 tablespoons plus 2 teaspoons instant espresso powder
3 heaping tablespoons unsweetened cocoa
1¼ cups powdered nondairy creamer
½ cup sugar
2 teaspoons cinnamon

In a bowl or plastic bag, stir together the espresso powder, cocoa, nondairy creamer, sugar, and cinnamon. Simply store tightly covered until needed. You can substitute decaffeinated instant coffee for the espresso . You can also replace the cocoa with Café Vienna instant coffee or another of your favorites.

Ginger Beer

Makes 1 gallon

1½ cups sugar
2 ounces grated ginger root
Zest and juice from 1 lemon
1 gallon boiling water
1 tablespoon yeast

Combine the sugar, grated ginger, and the lemon zest in a large bowl. Pour boiling water over top. Let cool until lukewarm, then strain. Add the lemon juice and the yeast and let stand overnight. Stir thoroughly, and pour into jars with tight-fitting lids or corks. Store in the refrigerator until you need it.

Faux Absinthe

Makes 1 pint

2 teaspoons dried wormwood
1 pint vodka
2 teaspoons chopped angelica root
2 teaspoons crushed anise seed
4 crushed cardamom pods
½ teaspoon crushed fennel seed
½ teaspoon ground coriander
1 teaspoon marjoram

Put wormwood in a bowl and pour vodka over top. Let steep for two days. Strain vodka thoroughly, return to bowl, and add remaining herbs. Let sit for one week, then strain and bottle. Serve in a cordial glass with a sugar cube.

Spiced Cider

Makes 1 gallon

1 gallon apple cider
1 teaspoon allspice
½ teaspoon
    ground cinnamon
½ teaspoon ground cloves
1 cinnamon stick

Cider is tarter then just plain apple juice. It is made from early-harvest apples, which have a lower sugar content. For a yummy treat, try adding Tuaca to a cup of spiced cider topped with whipped cream.

Pour all the ingredients into a pot and simmer for one hour. You can also put everything into a Crock-Pot™ or slow cooker and set on warm. Experiment by adding ¼ cup of any of these other ingredients: real maple syrup, honey, white wine, or white grape juice. Serve warm.

Mulled Wine

Serves 8

2 bottles red wine
2 ounces sugar
2 teaspoons honey
2 sliced lemons
Pinch ground cloves
1 stick cinnamon
2 pinches grated nutmeg
1 cup water

Bring the water and sugar to a boil, then remove from heat. Add the wine, honey, cloves, and cinnamon. Reheat without boiling for 5 minutes. Pour over the sliced lemon, and top with the grated nutmeg. Serve warm. This wine is a popular drink for the holidays.

Balloon Wine

Makes 5 bottles

¼ teaspoon dry yeast
4 cups sugar
1 gallon distilled water
1 thick toy punching balloon
1 large can thawed frozen grape juice
1 large can thawed frozen apple juice

Making homemade wine properly involves lots of wine-making tools and utensils. This simple recipe anyone can make. You are allowed by law to make as much homemade wine as you wish. You just cannot sell it.

Mix the juice, yeast, and sugar. Funnel into a glass gallon jug and fill with distilled water. Fit the balloon over the mouth of the jug and secure with string. Set the jug in a dark place for three weeks. The balloon will inflate and then deflate again. When the balloon goes limp, pour out the wine, being careful not to disturb the sediment. Bottle and chill.

Wine Coolers

Makes 1 drink

Wine of your choice
Citrus- or fruit-flavored soda of your choice

Wine coolers are easy to make. Half-fill a tall glass of ice with wine, then fill with Sprite, 7-Up, Fresca, or your favorite. Make this a low-calorie/carb treat by using diet flavored sodas, like these choices from Diet Rite: tangerine, raspberry, golden peach, black cherry, kiwi strawberry, or white grape.

Mead

Makes 4 quarts

1 gallon water
2½ pounds honey
Juice from 1 lemon
½ tablespoon nutmeg
1 package ale or champagne yeast

Mead has a long history. Some say that it may be well the oldest-recorded fermented drink. It has even been discovered in archeological digs. It lost its popularity when sugar became cheaply available in the eighteenth century.

Boil the water and honey, then add the lemon juice and nutmeg. Skim any foam that rises to the surface. Let cool to room temperature, then add the yeast. Cover and let sit at room temperature for 17 days—any longer, and the fermenting yeast will make the mixture explosive. Bottle in glass containers with tight lids or corks, and let age for two weeks. Refrigerate.

Hot Buttered Rum Mix

Serves 25

3 cups brown sugar
½ cup butter
2 tablespoons honey
1 tablespoon rum extract
1 tablespoon vanilla extract
½ teaspoon ground nutmeg
1 teaspoon ground cinnamon
½ teaspoon ground allspice

Beat the butter in a mixer until creamy. Add brown sugar and beat again until fluffy. Add honey, rum extract, and vanilla extract; beat, then add nutmeg, cinnamon, and allspice. Beat until sugar is dissolved and mixture is very light and smooth. Store refrigerated in a jar with a tight lid. You can also freeze mixture halfway in an ice cube tray—store frozen in a freezer bag, and pop one out when needed. To make Hot Buttered Rum with this recipe, simply pour 1½ ounces of light or dark rum into a coffee mug. Add a spoonful of the mix, and fill with hot water.

chapter 11

Traditional Cocktails Everyone Should Know

Blue Hawaiian

Makes 1 drink

1 ounce light rum
1 ounce blue curaçao
Pineapple juice
Sweet-n-sour mix
Pineapple slice, maraschino cherry, paper parasol

Fill a tall glass with ice. Pour in the rum and blue curaçao, then add the pineapple juice and sweet-n-sour mix in equal amounts. Garnish with a cherry-speared pineapple slice and a tropical parasol.

Cape Cod

Makes 1 drink

1 ounce vodka
Cranberry juice

This simple yet popular drink has only two ingredients. As a result, the Cape Cod can make a strong foundation for many other drinks. If you use equal parts of cranberry and grapefruit juice, you make a Seabreeze. Equal parts of cranberry and pineapple juice make a Baybreeze. Add an ounce of peach schnapps to a Cape Cod, and you have a Woo Woo.

Fill a glass with ice. Pour in the vodka, then fill with cranberry juice. Some people like to garnish it with a lime. Try different flavored vodkas mixed with cranberry juice for a different taste—lemon- or orange-flavored vodka would work well.

Fuzzy Navel

Makes 1 drink

1½ ounces peach schnapps
Orange juice

The Fuzzy Navel became popular in the early 1980s when Peachtree schnapps hit the market. Since then, this popular and delectable liqueur has become a common ingredient in many cocktails as a way of adding a hint of peach flavor.

Pour the peach schnapps into a glass of ice and fill to the top with orange juice. To make a Hairy Navel, add an ounce of vodka. (If you replace the orange juice with equal parts of orange juice and cranberry juice, then you've made a Sex on the Beach!)

Cosmopolitan

Makes 1 drink

1½ ounces vodka
½ ounce triple sec
¼ ounce lime juice
¼ ounce cranberry juice

Pour all the ingredients into a shaker tin of ice, then shake and strain into a cocktail glass. To upgrade, use a premium vodka and Cointreau in place of the triple sec. You can also use flavored vodkas to vary the taste—raspberry- and lemon-flavored vodka are good ones to try.

Greyhound

Makes 1 drink

1½ ounces vodka
Grapefruit juice

Fill a glass of your choice with ice. Pour in the vodka, then fill with grapefruit juice. This drink also tastes great with pink grapefruit juice; some people like to add a little bit of grenadine to sweeten it up. If you salt the rim of the glass, then this drink becomes a Salty Dog.

· ·

Kamikaze

Makes 1 drink

1½ ounces vodka
½ ounce triple sec
¼ ounce lime juice

Pour all the ingredients into a shaker tin of ice. Shake, then strain into a cocktail glass. You can also serve this on the rocks. Add some cranberry juice, and you have a Cosmopolitan.

Lemondrop

Makes 1 drink

1½ ounces vodka

½ ounce triple sec

3 ounces sweet-n-sour mix

Sugar

Lemon wedge

> Try Grand Marnier in this recipe instead of triple sec. You can also vary the garnish by pouring the sugar over the lemon, then the Grand Marnier over that, and then lighting. The sugar melts into the lemon. Bite into the warm sugary lemon slice after drinking the Lemondrop.

Rub the lemon around the rim of a cocktail glass. Dip the rim and the lemon slice into sugar. Pour vodka, triple sec, and sweet-n-sour mix into a shaker tin of ice. Shake, then strain into the sugar-rimmed glass. Raw sugar makes an interesting change, and a lemon-flavored vodka is a nice touch.

Long Island Tea

Makes 1 drink

½ ounce vodka

½ ounce gin

½ ounce rum

½ ounce tequila

½ ounce triple sec

3 ounces sweet-n-sour mix

Cola

Select a tall glass and fill to the brim with ice. Add all the ingredients, topping with a splash of cola, and stir well. You'll be amazed how much this tastes like actual iced tea. Substitute cranberry juice for the cola, and you have a Long Beach Tea.

Manhattan

Makes 1 drink

2 ounces whiskey
1 ounce sweet vermouth
2 dashes Angostura bitters
Maraschino cherry

It is believed that the bartender at a party thrown by Winston Churchill's mother invented the Manhattan. The party was at the Manhattan Club in New York City. Replace the whiskey with scotch, and this drink is called a Rob Roy.

Manhattans can be served straight up or on the rocks. Shake and strain the ingredients into a cocktail glass or pour them into a glass of ice. Garnish with a cherry. Add some cherry juice to make a sweet Manhattan. To make a perfect Manhattan, use half dry and half sweet vermouth.

Margarita

Makes 1 drink

1½ ounces tequila
½ ounce triple sec
½ ounce fresh-squeezed lime juice
Sweet-n-sour mix to taste
Lime wedge
Kosher salt

Rub lime slice around the rim of a margarita glass (or just half the rim) and dip rim in kosher salt. Pour tequila, triple sec, lime juice, and sweet-n-sour mix into a shaker tin of ice. Shake, then strain into the glass. In addition to straight up, margaritas can be served frozen or on the rocks. Feel free to play around with different types of tequila. Try replacing the triple sec with Cointreau or Grand Marnier or with another flavoring, like melon liqueur.

Martini

Makes 1 drink

2 ounces gin
1/8 ounce dry vermouth
2 big pimento-stuffed green olives

Chill the gin and dry vermouth ahead of time in refrigerator or freezer. Pour gin and vermouth into shaker tin of ice. Shake or stir, and strain into in a chilled martini glass. Leave out the vermouth, and you have a very dry martini. Add more vermouth, and you have a wet martini. Add olive juice, and you have made a dirty martini.

Mimosa

Makes 1 drink

Anyone who's ever eaten brunch has probably had a Mimosa. It is by far the most popular brunch cocktail ever.

Fresh-squeezed orange juice
Champagne
Strawberry half

Fill a fluted Champagne glass one quarter of the way with orange juice. Fill the glass the rest of the way with champagne, and garnish the rim with a strawberry. Save the strawberry for last—the glass will topple if you try to prep the rim beforehand.

Piña Colada

Makes 1 drink

1½ ounces light rum
3 ounces pineapple juice
1 ounce Coco Lopez
Slice of pineapple (peeled and cored)

Put all the ingredients into a blender with some ice. Blend until smooth. Dark rum is yummy in place of the light. Some people like more coconut flavor than pineapple, so play around with the measures. Add half-and-half and vanilla extract to enhance the flavor. Replace the rum with vodka, and this drink is called a Chi Chi.

- -

Purple Hooter

Makes 1 drink

1½ ounces vodka
1 ounce raspberry liqueur
1 ounce pineapple juice
1 ounce sweet-n-sour mix

Pour all the ingredients into a shaker tin of ice. Shake, then strain into a cocktail glass of your choice. Before shooting it down, hold this shooter up to your nose—it smells like candy. Experiment with different flavored vodkas, like currant, raspberry, or strawberry.

Rusty Nail

Makes 1 drink

1½ ounces Scotch whiskey
½ ounce Drambuie

A Rusty Nail is served on the rocks. Fill a rocks glass with ice, and pour in the ingredients. The Drambuie is a perfect complement to the Scotch whiskey because Drambuie is a Scotch-based honey liqueur. Some people like to add a bit more or less Drambuie to their Rusty Nail.

• •

Screwdriver

Makes 1 drink

1½ ounces vodka
Fresh-squeezed orange juice

It is said that the drink called the Screwdriver was invented in the 1950s by American oil-rig workers who were stationed in the Middle East. They stirred this creation with the screwdrivers that hung on their belts.

Fill a glass with ice. Pour in the vodka and add the orange juice to fill. If you add equal parts of cranberry and orange juice, it's called a Madras. Add peach schnapps, and you have a Hairy Navel. Add sloe gin, and you've made a Sloe Screw. Add Galliano, and you have made a Harvey Wallbanger.

Sloe Screw

Makes 1 drink

1 ounce vodka
1 ounce sloe gin
Fresh orange juice

The Sloe Screw is part of the screwdriver family. Sloe gin is used, a liqueur that has no gin in it whatsoever. Red and sweet, it's flavored with blackthorn sloe plums and aged in wood barrels.

Put all the ingredients into a tall glass of ice and stir. Add an ounce of Southern Comfort, and you've made a Sloe Comfortable Screw. Add some Galliano to the Sloe Comfortable Screw, and you have made yourself a Sloe Comfortable Screw up Against the Wall. See how that works?

Tequila Sunrise

Makes 1 drink

1½ ounces tequila
½ ounce grenadine
Orange juice

Fill a tall glass with ice, then add ingredients one at a time and in order. The grenadine is very heavy and will fall to the bottom of the glass, creating a sunrise effect. Try upgrading to gold tequila and, whenever possible, using fresh-squeezed orange juice. It will make a big difference.

Tom Collins

Makes 1 drink

1½ ounces gin
2 ounces sweet-n-sour mix
Club soda or Sprite
Orange slice and a maraschino cherry

Fill a Collins glass or any other tall glass with ice. Pour in the gin, sweet-n-sour mix, and the club soda or Sprite. A Tom Collins should have a frothy top, so pour the contents of the glass into an empty shaker tin and give it a couple of shakes, then pour it back into the glass. Garnish with the orange and cherry.

- -

White Russian

Makes 1 drink

1 ounce vodka
1 ounce coffee liqueur
Half-and-half or milk

Most people think that a White Russian tastes just like chocolate milk. Leave out the half-and-half or milk, and you have made a Black Russian. There are different measures for the vodka/coffee liqueur ratio. Experiment to your taste.

Fill a cocktail glass of your choice with ice. Add the vodka, coffee liqueur, and half-and-half or milk. Stir. Add Irish cream liqueur to make a Mudslide. Replace the vodka with amaretto, and you have a Toasted Almond. Add Irish cream to a Toasted Almond, and you have an Orgasm. Add vodka to an Orgasm, and you have made yourself a Screaming Orgasm.

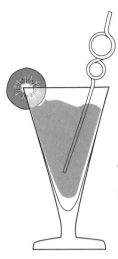

chapter 12

Pure Nonalcoholic Mocktails

Sweet and Innocent Cooler

Makes 1 drink

4 ounces Ariel
Nonalcoholic wine
    of your choice
Diet Rite white grape soda
Sprig of grapes

Ariel is a pioneer in producing award-winning nonalcoholic wines. It even won a gold medal in a blind tasting against wines with alcohol. Ariel has been producing nonalcoholic wine with its patented process since 1985.

Pour the nonalcoholic wine into a tall glass of ice. Fill with Diet Rite white grape soda and stir. You can replace the soda with ginger ale, Sprite, or 7-Up, but the white grape soda has a great flavor that mixes with the nonalcoholic wine nicely.

Like a Blessed Blackberry Virgin

Makes 1 drink

Handful of blackberries
Spoon of sugar or Splenda
Lemonade
Lemon and blackberries for garnish

Put the blackberries and sugar or Splenda in the blender. Blend until smooth, then pour into a tall glass. Pack the glass with ice, and fill with lemonade. Garnish with a lemon slice and some blackberries. For a really great-tasting drink, make your own fresh-squeezed lemonade.

Touched by a Fuzzy Angel

Makes 1 drink

1 ounce Torani peach syrup
Orange juice
Orange or peach slice

Pour the peach syrup into a tall glass of ice, then fill with orange juice. This drink can also be made frozen. Just blend all ingredients. If you would like it smooth and creamy, add some half-and-half while blending. Garnish with an orange or peach slice.

Virgin Island Seabreeze

Makes 1 drink

1 part pink grapefruit juice
1 part cranberry juice
Lime slice for garnish

You can vary this drink to your heart's content. To make a Virgin Island Baybreeze, simply replace the grapefruit juice with pineapple juice and garnish with a pineapple slice. Jazz it up by using the different flavors of cranberry juices that are available.

Fill a tall glass with ice and then pour in equal amounts of the pink grapefruit juice and cranberry juice to the top of the glass. Garnish with a slice of lime. You can substitute the pink grapefruit juice for regular grapefruit juice if you prefer a tarter taste.

Nada Colada

Makes 1 drink

¼ ounce rum extract
¼ ounce vanilla extract
3 ounces pineapple juice
3 ounces Coco Lopez
Milk or half-and-half
Pineapple slice and maraschino cherry

Pour the rum extract, vanilla extract, pineapple juice, and Coco Lopez into a blender with a cup of ice. Add milk or half-and-half and blend until a smooth consistency as been reached. Pour into a tall glass, and garnish with a pineapple slice and maraschino cherry. The rum extract can be omitted if desired.

* *

Big as the Moon Pie

Makes 1 drink

2 scoops banana ice cream
Half-and-half
4 vanilla wafers
Whipped cream

A Chattanooga bakery conceived the MoonPie in the early 1900s. It was developed for the local miners, who wanted a snack that fit in their lunch pails. They wanted something that was solid and filling.

Crush three of the vanilla wafers and put into a tall glass. Blend the banana ice cream in a blender, adding half-and-half little by little to reach a smooth consistency. Pour into the glass and garnish with whipped cream and the fourth vanilla wafer.

Blushin' Berry Mary

Makes 1 drink

½ cup fresh raspberries
½ cup strawberry milk
1 cup lemon yogurt
½ cup milk
Whipped cream, strawberries, blueberries, and raspberries for garnish

Put the fresh raspberries, strawberry milk, lemon yogurt, and milk in a blender. Blend until smooth, then pour into a tall glass. Garnish with whipped cream, strawberries, blueberries, and raspberries. Substitute a different flavored yogurt if you desire. Seasonal fruit can replace the berry garnish.

Vow of Chastity on the Beach

Makes 1 drink

1 ounce Torani peach syrup
Equal parts of orange juice
and cranberry juice
Orange slice and a cherry

The cocktail Sex on the Beach came out in the early 1980s when DeKuyper Peachtree schnapps hit the market. Even today it is still one of the most popular drinks served.

Fill a tall glass with ice. Pour in the peach syrup, then fill with equal parts of orange juice and cranberry juice. This drink can also be served frozen. If you want it peachier, simply add more peach syrup. Garnish with an orange or peach slice and a cherry.

Mother Theresa Tea

Makes 1 drink

5 ounces chai tea mix
2 scoops vanilla ice cream
Milk or half-and-half
Cinnamon stick

Put the chai tea mix and the vanilla ice cream in a blender. Slowly add the milk or half-and-half until you've reached a smooth consistency. Pour into a tall glass and garnish with a cinnamon stick. If you prefer a thicker drink, add ice cubes during the blending process.

Morally Pure Mudslide

Makes 1 drink

1 scoop chocolate ice cream
1 scoop vanilla ice cream
1 ounce black coffee
2 spoons of Café Vienna (General Foods International Coffee)
1 ounce chocolate syrup
Milk or half-and-half to blend

This is a nonalcoholic version of a frozen cocktail called a Mudslide. A really cool way to present it is to twirl and lace the chocolate inside of the glass before pouring in the mixture.

Put the chocolate ice cream, vanilla ice cream, coffee, Café Vienna, and chocolate syrup into a blender. Blend, adding milk or half-and-half little by little until smooth. Pour into a tall glass. To make the drink thicker, you can add cubes of ice while blending.

Cool as a Cucumber

Makes 1 drink

Half a cucumber, peeled
Juice from half a lime
2 mint leaves
Half a ripe kiwi, peeled
2 spoons of sugar or Splenda
Sprig of mint for garnish

Put the cucumber, lime juice, mint leaves, kiwi, and sugar in a blender with a cup of ice. Blend until smooth. You may have to add a little water to the mix. Pour into a glass of your choice, then garnish with a sprig of mint. This is a very refreshing summertime drink.

Mango Virgo

Makes 1 drink

3 ounces mango nectar
Juice from half a lime
2 ounces half-and-half
Star fruit

Pour the mango nectar, lime juice, and half-and-half into a shaker tin of ice. Shake, and strain into a chilled martini glass. Garnish rim with a slice of star fruit. If you prefer this cocktail a little sweeter, simply spoon some Splenda on top—it dissolves quickly.

Wild Blueberry Beginner

Makes 1 drink

5 mint leaves
Handful of blueberries
2 spoons of sugar or Splenda
1 ounce water
7-Up
Sprig of mint and a few blueberries

Put the mint leaves, blueberries, sugar or Splenda, and water in a tall glass. Mash all the ingredients together with a muddler or wooden spoon to release the flavor from the mint. Fill the glass with ice. Pour in 7-Up to fill, and garnish with mint and blueberries.

· ·

Coconut Catholic Schoolgirl

Makes 1 drink

3 ounces Coco Lopez
Juice from 1 lime
Spoonful of honey
Shredded coconut

In the words of Harry Nilsson: Brother bought a coconut, he bought it for a dime, his sister had another, she paid it for a lime. She put the lime in the coconut, and drank them both up.

Prep a martini glass by dipping the rim into honey, then into the shredded coconut to create a fun coconut rim. Pour the Coco Lopez and lime juice into a shaker tin of ice. Shake, then strain into the martini glass. Chill the glass in the freezer to add a nice touch.

Just Say No Cocoa

Makes 1 drink

1 packet hot cocoa mix
3/4 cup hot water
Eggnog
Whipped cream

Eggnog, with its European roots, soon became a popular wintertime drink throughout colonial America. President George Washington was a big fan of eggnog and devised his own recipe, which included rye whiskey, rum, and sherry.

Pour a packet of hot cocoa mix into a mug. Fill three quarters of the way with very hot water, then stir well. Fill the rest of the way with eggnog and top with whipped cream. If you don't like the whipped cream, you can top it off with miniature marshmallows.

Ain't Misbehavin' Mary

Makes 1 drink

V-8 juice
Juice from 1 lime slice
Juice from 1 lemon slice
Dash Tabasco (optional)
½ teaspoon A-1 steak sauce (optional)
Dash Worcestershire sauce (optional)
½ teaspoon raw horseradish (optional)
Celery stalk (optional)
1 large green olive (optional)

Fill a tall glass with V-8 juice. (Regular tomato juice can be substituted.) Add the juice from a lime slice and the juice from a lemon slice. The rest of the ingredients are optional and depend on your taste preferences.

Good Ship Lollipop

Makes 1 drink

3 small cantaloupe balls
3 small watermelon balls
1 large scoop of orange sherbet
Cold Diet Rite Golden Peach soda or Nehi Peach soda

Drop a large scoop of orange sherbet into the bottom of a tall glass. Fill with cold Diet Rite Golden Peach soda or Nehi Peach soda, then drop in the cantaloupe and watermelon balls. You can replace the orange sherbet with pineapple or lime if you desire.

Sweet Sunrise

Makes 1 drink

Orange juice
½ ounce grenadine
Orange slice

Fill a tall glass with ice, then fill with orange juice. Slowly pour the grenadine into the drink—it will sink to the bottom of the glass, making a sunrise effect. Garnish with an orange or peach slice. Fresh-squeezed orange juice would be a nice touch.

Earth Angel Sangria

Makes 1 drink

3/4 glass grape juice
Club soda
Orange wheel, lime wheel,
pineapple slice, and a cherry for garnish

To make this nonalcoholic sangria, you can use purple grape juice or white grape juice. You can also replace the juice with nonalcoholic wine if you desire. Just make sure you garnish with all kinds of seasonal fruit.

Fill a tall glass three quarters of the way with grape juice. Fill with soda water, then garnish with an orange wheel, lime wheel, pineapple slice, and a cherry. Make this sangria for a party by simply increasing the amounts and serving in a pitcher or punch bowl.

chapter 13

Quick and Easy Finger Foods

Chinese Three Slivers

Cocktail
Complement:
Good Karmatini
(page 16)

Serves 4

1 tablespoon vegetable oil

1 4-ounce can sliced bamboo shoots, drained and rinsed

8 ounces (about 3 cakes) hard tofu,
   sliced into ¼-inch strips, patted dry with paper towel

1 package enoki mushrooms, roots trimmed, washed,
   and broken into individual strands

¼ cup Asian dumpling dipping sauce

½ teaspoon sambal or other Asian chili paste (optional)

1 tablespoon cornstarch dissolved in 2 tablespoons cold water

1 head iceberg lettuce

1. Heat the oil in a skillet or wok until very hot but not smoking. Add the bamboo shoots, and stir for 1 minute. Slide the tofu into the pan, and cook over high heat without stirring until lightly browned. Add the enoki mushrooms, dumpling sauce, chili paste, and cornstarch solution. Cook until thick, about 2 minutes. Transfer to a serving bowl.

2. Select 4 unbroken leaves from the lettuce head; wash thoroughly and tear them in half.

3. Place the bowl of cooked Chinese vegetables in the center of a large serving platter, and arrange the lettuce pieces around the bowl. Guests can spoon filling into the leaves and eat the lettuce-wraps with their hands. Extra sauces aren't needed on the side because the vegetables provide enough flavor.

Simple Salsa

Cocktail Complement:
Tasting Away in Margaritaville (page 30)

Yields 1 cup

2 large tomatoes
1 small onion, finely diced
1 or 2 jalapeño peppers, finely chopped
½ teaspoon fresh-squeezed lime juice
Handful of cilantro leaves, cleaned and roughly chopped
Salt and freshly ground black pepper

1. Quarter the tomatoes. Discard the seeds and cut into a fine dice.
2. Toss together with the diced onion, jalapeños, lime juice, cilantro, salt, and pepper. Keeps in the refrigerator for 2 days, but is best used the day it's made.

Salsa Story

Tomato story: In 1883, a tomato importer named John Nix was upset that the United States Congress passed a 10 percent tariff on all imported vegetables. He set out to prove that tomatoes were technically not a vegetable but a fruit that was grown on a vine—and he won. To this day, thanks to Mr. Nix, taxes are not paid on imported tomatoes.

Fairy-Tale Fondue

Serves 6

1 garlic clove, halved

2 cups dry white wine

3/4 pound Emmental (Swiss) cheese,
   shredded (about 3 cups)

3/4 pound Gruyère cheese, shredded (about 3 cups)

1 tablespoon cornstarch

2 tablespoons kirsch

Assorted steamed vegetables such as carrot sticks,
   broccoli, cauliflower, and green beans

Cubes of French bread, marbled rye and pumpernickel, and pumpkin bread

Cocktail
Complement:

Rimmed Brothers
Grimm Cocoa
(page 79)

1. Rub the inside of a medium saucepot with the cut side of the garlic. Discard the clove (or leave it in, if you prefer). Add the wine, and place pot over medium heat until wine simmers. Whisk in the cheese in small handfuls, making sure that the each addition has completely melted before adding the next. Combine the cornstarch and kirsch into a paste; whisk into cheese mixture. Simmer the fondue gently for 5 to 7 minutes and allow the cornstarch to thicken.

2. Transfer the cheese mixture to a fondue pot, and set a low flame under it—just enough to keep it at the border of simmering. Serve with the vegetables and bread for dipping.

Far, Far Away

Emmental and Gruyère cheeses are from the enchanting country of Switzerland. They are excellent for fondue. Create a fairy-tale presentation with Little Red Riding Hood's basket of goodies tipped with spilled colorful vegetables and cubes of pumpkin, marbled, and French bread.

Pico de Gallo

Serves 8

4 medium tomatoes, seeded
and diced fine (about 1½ cups)
2 small white onions, finely chopped
1 jalapeño pepper, seeded and finely chopped
1 tablespoon puréed chipotle in adobo sauce
½ teaspoon salt
2 teaspoons lime juice
¼ cup chopped cilantro

Cocktail
Complement:
Swim-up Bar Margarita
(page 26)

In a blender or food processor, purée ½ cup of the tomatoes. Combine with remaining tomatoes, onions, jalapeños, chipotle, salt, lime juice, and cilantro. Best if used within 2 days.

Hot and Homemade

Chipotle in adobo: 6 or 7 dried chipotle chilies (smoked and dried jalapeño peppers) slit lengthwise and seeds removed, 1½ cups water, ¼ teaspoon salt, ¼ medium onion sliced, 1 clove garlic diced, 3 tablespoons ketchup, and 1/8 cup apple cider vinegar. Simmer in a covered pan for one hour and stir occasionally. Store in fridge.

Spiced Pecans

Yields 3 cups

1 ounce (2 tablespoons) unsalted butter
1 pound whole, shelled pecans
2 tablespoons light soy sauce
1 tablespoon hoisin sauce
A few drops of hot pepper sauce

Cocktail
Complement:
Honeymoon Suitetini
(page 19)

1. Heat oven to 325°F. Melt butter in a large skillet. Add nuts and cook, tossing occasionally, until nuts are well coated. Add soy sauce, hoisin sauce, and hot pepper sauce; cook 1 minute more. Stir to coat thoroughly.
2. Spread nuts into a single layer on a baking sheet. Bake until all liquid is absorbed and nuts begin to brown. Remove from oven. Cool before serving.

Party Pecans

Spiced Pecans are great to serve around the room in little bowls with napkins beside them. Pecans are normally considered a winter season appetizer, but since they are available in the baking aisle of any grocery store all year round, you can serve them any time of the year that you desire.

Spicy White Bean Sunshine Dip

Serves 12

Cocktail
Complement:
Tequila Sunrise
Margarita
(page 33)

2 15-ounce cans white navy beans, drained and rinsed
¼ cup sour cream
1 tablespoon orange juice concentrate
1 teaspoon chipotle purée
1 teaspoon lime juice
Zest of 1 orange, grated
½ teaspoon salt
½ cup diced white onions
1 tablespoon chopped cilantro

1. Purée the beans, sour cream, orange juice concentrate, chipotle, lime juice, orange zest, and salt in a food processor until smooth.
2. Add onions and cilantro; mix with a rubber spatula until combined.

Ancient Aztec Dip

Chipotles are a Mexican specialty—smoked jalapeño chili peppers. The Aztecs smoked jalapeño peppers because they were hard to dry and prone to rot. Smoking allowed the Aztecs to store the peppers longer. Today, as much as a fifth of the Mexican jalapeño crop is processed into chipotles and sold all over the world.

Simple Hummus

Cocktail Complement:

Hunka Hunka Burnin' Love (page 60)

Yields 2 cups

1 cup dried garbanzos (chickpeas)
   soaked overnight if desired, or 1 16-ounce can
2 cloves garlic, peeled
3 tablespoons tahini
½ teaspoon kosher salt
2–3 teaspoons toasted cumin powder
Juice of 1 lemon, divided in half
¼ cup extra-virgin olive oil, plus a little extra for garnish
Freshly ground black pepper
Paprika and chopped parsley for garnish (optional)
Pita bread for dipping

1. If using dried chickpeas, cook them in lightly salted water until very, very tender. If using canned chickpeas, drain and rinse them. In a food processor, chop the garlic until it sticks to the sides of the bowl. Add chickpeas, tahini, salt, cumin, and half of the lemon juice. Process until smooth, gradually drizzling in the olive oil. Add up to ¼ cup cold water to achieve a softer hummus if desired. Season to taste with black pepper, and additional salt and lemon to taste.

2. Spread onto plates and garnish with a drizzle of extra-virgin olive oil, a few drops of lemon, a dusting of paprika, and some chopped parsley. Serve with wedges of warm pita bread.

Garbanzo Butter

Peanuts are to peanut butter what sesame is to tahini. Tahini can be used as a sandwich spread, like peanut butter, or it can be mixed with a variety of other seasonings such as garlic, onion, and cayenne pepper for a tasty dip or salad dressing. You almost always find it as a key ingredient in hummus.

Capellini Pancetta Frittata

Serves 10–12 as an appetizer

¼ pound capellini, broken into ½-inch lengths
1 tablespoon salt
4 eggs, beaten
1 cup shredded mozzarella
Salt and freshly ground black pepper to taste
Pinch dried hot red pepper flakes
6 thick slices pancetta, cut into small pieces and cooked until crisp
1 cup frozen tiny peas, thawed
1/3 cup freshly grated Parmesan cheese
1 tablespoon olive oil
3 cloves garlic, crushed

Cocktail Complement:

Upside-Down Pineapple Martini
(page 21)

1. In a large pot, bring at least 3 quarts of water to a rolling boil. Add the salt. Add the capellini and stir to prevent sticking. Cook until al dente. Drain.
2. In a medium bowl, combine the eggs, cooked capellini, mozzarella, and salt and pepper to taste. Add red pepper flakes and mix well.
3. In another bowl, gently combine the cooked pancetta, peas, and Parmesan.
4. In a 10-inch nonstick skillet, heat the oil over medium heat. Add the garlic and sauté about 1 minute, until softened. Pour half the egg and pasta mixture into the skillet and top with the pancetta mixture. Cover with the remaining pasta mixture. Cook 8 or 9 minutes, pressing down slightly. Invert the frittata onto a plate.
5. Add more oil to the skillet, if necessary, and return the frittata to pan, uncooked side down. Cook until golden, about 5 more minutes. Cut into small wedges and serve.

Son-in-Law Eggs

Serves 10

¼ cup vegetable oil

10 hard-boiled eggs, cooled and peeled

2 shallots, thinly sliced

1/3 cup light brown sugar

3 tablespoons fish sauce

1/3 cup tamarind concentrate

¼ cup chopped cilantro

Dried hot chili flakes to taste

Cocktail
Complement:
Branded Buttery Nipple
(page 63)

1. Heat the vegetable oil in a skillet over medium heat. Place the whole eggs in the skillet and fry until golden brown. Remove the eggs to paper towels and set aside. (If your skillet can't hold all of the eggs comfortably, do this in batches.)
2. Add the shallots to the skillet and sauté until just beginning to brown. Remove the shallots from the oil with a slotted spoon and set aside.
3. Put the brown sugar, fish sauce, and tamarind concentrate in the skillet. Stir to combine, and bring to a simmer. Cook the mixture, stirring constantly, until the sauce thickens, about 5 minutes; remove from heat.
4. Cut the eggs in half vertically and place them face-up on a rimmed serving dish. Spread the shallots over the eggs, and then drizzle the eggs with the sauce. Garnish with cilantro and chili pepper flakes.

Tamarind Find

Tamarind concentrate can be found in Asian stores, natural stores, and sometimes in the international aisle of your local grocery store. Tamarind is a fruit that grows on tamarind trees in Southeast Asia. You could make your own concentrate from the pods, but it's too time-consuming to do so.

Rice Paper Rolls

Serves 2–4

1 cup thin rice noodles
8–10 medium to large cooked shrimp, cut in half
4 sheets of rice spring-roll wrapper (8 x 10 inches)
1 cup grated carrot
1 small cucumber, shredded
20 mint leaves

Cocktail Complement:

The Frog Prince in a Blender (page 78)

1. Soak the rice noodles in very hot water until they are soft, usually 10 to 20 minutes; drain. You can leave the noodles whole, or cut them into 2-inch pieces if you prefer.
2. Place a clean kitchen towel on a work surface with a bowl of hot water nearby. Put a sheet of the rice spring-roll wrapper in the hot water for approximately 20 seconds, just until soft; lay it out on the towel.
3. In the middle of the spring-roll wrapper, place 2 to 3 pieces of shrimp and ¼ of the noodles, carrots, and cucumbers. Top with mint.
4. Quickly roll up the spring-roll wrapper, keeping it fairly tight; then roll up the whole thing in plastic wrap, making sure to keep it tight. Refrigerate until ready to serve.

Asian Party

Serve the rolls at an Asian-themed party. Invitations can be written on a chopstick, on a note in a fortune cookie, or on a note in a Chinese take out container. Look for Micron pens at craft stores so you can write finely on the chopstick.

Southwestern Apricot Salsa

○ ○ ○ ○ ○
Cocktail
Complement:
South of the Peachy
Border Rita
(page 31)

Serves 12–24

2 tablespoons red onion, chopped
½ teaspoon fresh jalapeño pepper, minced
2 cups canned apricots in light syrup, chopped
½ tablespoon olive oil
1 tablespoon fresh cilantro
½ teaspoon white vinegar
½ tablespoon lime juice
¼ teaspoon lime peel, grated
¼ teaspoon ground cumin
½ teaspoon garlic salt
½ teaspoon ground white pepper

1. Peel and chop the onion into ¼-inch pieces. Remove the stem from jalapeño pepper and mince. Drain and rinse the apricots and cut into ¼-inch pieces.
2. Combine all the ingredients in the slow cooker. Cook uncovered on low setting for 1 to 2 hours.

Got Apricot?

This is a great dip for a Western party! You can serve the Southwestern Apricot Salsa with plain tortilla chips, or try tricolored or lime-flavored chips for an added burst of flavor. How about putting the chips in upside-down cowboy hats? Maybe decorate with hay bales, old guitars, horseshoes, and rope.

Green Apple Salsa

Serves about 30

Cocktail Complement:
Caramel Appletini
(page 18)

6 large tomatoes
3 large, tart green apples
1 large Vidalia onion
1 large green bell pepper
1 large red bell pepper
1 small green jalapeño pepper
1 5-ounce can tomato paste
1½ cups packed brown sugar
1½ cups cider vinegar
½ teaspoon lime juice
2 tablespoons chili powder
2 teaspoons mustard seeds
½ teaspoon cayenne pepper
1 teaspoon salt
1 tablespoon V-8

1. Crush the tomatoes in the bottom of the slow cooker with a wooden spoon. Peel and chop the apples into ¼-inch pieces. Peel and chop the onion into ¼-inch pieces. Remove the stems and seeds from the green, red, and jalapeno peppers; chop into ¼-inch pieces.
2. Combine all the ingredients in the slow cooker and cook covered on low heat for 8 hours. If the sauce seems too runny, remove the cover for the last hour.

The World's Sweetest Onions

Vidalia onions are known as the world's sweetest onions. A man named Mose Coleman, who made a fortune on them in the Great Depression, first grew them in Toombs County, Georgia. The soil combined with climate makes the onions sweet. Today Georgia sells $90 million worth of Vidalia onions annually.

Li'l Baby Reubens

Cocktail Complement:

Cigar Band
(page 50)

Serves 12–24

½ pound corned beef
1 medium onion
1 16-ounce can sauerkraut
2 cups Swiss cheese, shredded
1 cup cheddar cheese, shredded
1 cup mayonnaise (do not substitute low-fat mayonnaise)
Thousand Island dressing
Rye crackers

1. Shred the corned beef with a fork. Peel and chop the onion into ¼-inch pieces. Drain and rinse the sauerkraut. Combine the corned beef, sauerkraut, Swiss cheese, onion, Cheddar cheese, and mayonnaise in the slow cooker. Cook covered on low setting for 2 hours, stirring every 15 minutes.
2. Serve on rye crackers with a small dollop of Thousand Island dressing.

Reuben Roulette

There are three stories competing for the truth about the inventor of the Reuben sandwich. One tells of a Manhattan delicatessen that claimed to serve the sandwich to Charlie Chaplin's leading lady in 1914. In another, a hotel in Omaha developed the sandwich to feed some late-night poker players in 1922. And in 1956, a waitress entered the sandwich in a contest and won.

Layered Mexican Dip

Cocktail Complement:

Mexican Flag (page 53)

Serves 8

3 medium-sized ripe avocados

2 tablespoons lemon juice

1 teaspoon salt

1 teaspoon garlic powder

½ cup sour cream

1 teaspoon chili powder

1 teaspoon onion salt

1 bunch green onions

3 medium-sized red tomatoes

1 cup black olives, pitted

½ pound Cheddar cheese

2 cups canned bean dip

1. Peel the avocados and remove the seeds. Mash together with the lemon juice, salt, and garlic powder. Set aside.
2. Mix together the sour cream, chili powder, and onion salt. Set aside.
3. Remove the roots from the green onions and chop into ½-inch pieces. Remove the stems from the tomatoes and cut into ½-inch pieces. Chop the black olives into ½-inch pieces. Grate the cheese.
4. Layer on a large plate or platter in the following order: bean dip, avocado mix, sour cream mix, onions, tomatoes, olives, cheese.
5. Cover and chill in the refrigerator for 4 hours before serving.

Big Show-Off

To really show off the layers, layer the dip in two clear bowls. This will bump up the presentation factor a few notches. Serve tricolored tortilla chips around the bowls of dip, making sure not to cover up the dip layers, or try raising the bowls by placing them on plates turned upside down and then adding the chips.

Mexican Roll-Ups

Cocktail Complement:

Hypnotizing Margarita
(page 28)

Serves 6

2 fresh jalapeño chili peppers
1 bunch green onions
½ cup black olives, pitted
16 ounces cream cheese
½ teaspoon garlic salt
½ teaspoon medium-hot red chili powder
6 flour tortillas

1. Remove the stems and seeds from the jalapeño peppers and chop the peppers into ¼-inch pieces. Remove the roots from the green onions and chop the onions and stems into ¼-inch pieces. Chop the olives into ¼-inch pieces.
2. Combine all the ingredients and mix until well blended.
3. Spread on tortillas. Roll up and serve.

South of the Border Party

Light up a south-of-the-border party with chili pepper lights. Hang the lights around the bar area and lay them around the food area. Inexpensive piñatas can liven up the room too. Miniature piñatas can be found at party stores and would be perfect to use as invitations. Simply put the invitations inside.

Spinach con Queso

Serves 8

1 10-ounce package frozen chopped spinach
1 small white onion
1 medium-sized red tomato
1 pound Velveeta cheese with jalapeños
½ cup whole milk
1 2-ounce jar diced pimientos

Cocktail Complement:

Uno Dos Tres Cuatro Cinco de Mayo Rita (page 28)

1. Thaw the spinach, and squeeze the water from it until as dry as possible.
2. Remove skin from the onion and chop into ¼-inch pieces. Chop the tomato into ¼-inch pieces.
3. Combine the onion, cheese, milk and pimientos in a medium-sized pot over low heat (or in a slow cooker set on the lowest temperature setting). Cook, stirring periodically, until the cheese melts. Stir in the spinach and tomato.

Bread Bowl Dip

To keep this dip warm, try serving Crock-Pot style set on low. Or for a really interesting presentation, make a large bread bowl. Hollow out a round of bread loaf, then set it in the middle of a platter. Pour the spinach con queso into the bread bowl and garnish with tortilla chips.

Mock Caviar

Cocktail
Complement:
Black Martini
(page 17)

Serves 12

1 eggplant (about 1 pound)
¼ cup olive oil
8 cloves garlic, skin on
3 tablespoons chopped parsley
Salt and freshly ground black pepper to taste

1. Preheat oven to 425°F.
2. Split the eggplant lengthwise and brush the cut surface with olive oil. Place on a baking sheet along with the whole garlic cloves. Bake for 30 to 40 minutes or until tender. Remove from oven and allow to cool.
3. Scoop out the flesh from the eggplant and transfer to the bowl of a food processor. Trim the root ends from the garlic cloves and squeeze out the garlic pulp; add the pulp to the eggplant. Add all the remaining ingredients and process until smooth. Store refrigerated in an airtight container.

Fake Caviar

Serve the mock caviar on an elegant platter with touches of gold or silver. Even a mirror can serve as a very nice platter. Try making crustless toasted white bread triangle points topped with cream cheese and a dollop of caviar. Garnish all around with piles of red onion, chopped boiled egg, capers, and chives.

Herbed Cheese Artichokes

Serves 15

1 can artichoke bottoms, rinsed and drained
8 ounces cream cheese, softened
2 tablespoons chopped fresh herbs (parsley, basil, chives, etc.)
Salt and freshly ground black pepper to taste
30 fresh radish slices

Cocktail Complement:

Southern Hospitality
Martini
(page 18)

1. Slice the artichoke bottoms into about 30 neatly trimmed slices. Mix together the cream cheese, herbs, and salt and pepper in a small bowl until smooth.
2. Use a pastry bag to pipe a small rosette of the cream cheese mixture (about 1 rounded tablespoon each) onto each artichoke slice. Top with a radish slice and serve immediately.

The Artichoke Queen

Interesting artichoke trivia: The artichoke dates back to A.D. 77 in Greek and Roman culture. It was first developed in Sicily. It was not until the early twentieth century that artichokes were grown in California. The most artichokes ever sold was during the year 1947. That was the year that Marilyn Monroe was named Artichoke Queen of Castroville, California, self-proclaimed Artichoke Capital of the World.

Spicy Jicama Chips

Serves 10

1 jicama, peeled, quartered, and thinly sliced
1/3 cup freshly squeezed lime juice
1 teaspoon chili powder
½ teaspoon ground red pepper
Salt to taste

⊙ Cocktail
Complement:
Key Lime Pie Margarita
(page 32)

1. Place the jicama slices in a shallow glass dish and toss with lime juice; allow to marinate for 30 minutes at room temperature.
2. Drain the chips. Sprinkle with chili powder, pepper, and salt.

Perky Chips

Place a bowl of your favorite dip in the middle of a colorful platter, then place the chips all around the bowl. For a nice presentation stick the last few chips point side up all around the bowl to create perky chip energy.

Ham Cornets

Serves 15

8 ounces cream cheese, softened
1 tablespoon Dijon mustard
2 tablespoons chopped fresh tarragon
Salt and freshly ground black pepper to taste
10 slices good-quality deli ham, cut into thirds
30 water crackers

Cocktail
Complement:
Cape Cod
(page 120)

1. Mix together the cream cheese, Dijon, tarragon, and salt and pepper in a small bowl until blended.
2. Place about 3/4 teaspoon of the cream cheese mixture at the short end of a ham slice and roll into a cornet shape. Repeat with the remaining slices, reserving a small amount of the cream cheese mixture.
3. To assemble, smear a very small amount of the cream cheese mixture on each cracker as a "glue" to secure the ham cornet. Top each cracker with the cornet and serve immediately.

Ham Display

Arrange the Ham Cornets on a solid-colored platter because the arrangement of the appetizer is a little busy, so you want to simplify the look. White, black, silver, or gold are nice choices. A tiered display would be a nice presentation as well or anything that you use to create levels—the eye is drawn to different levels.

Spinach and Ricotta Dip

Serves 12

1 10-ounce package frozen chopped spinach,
   thawed and drained
½ cup ricotta cheese
1/3 cup mayonnaise
¼ cup chopped green onions
¼ cup sour cream
3 tablespoons lemon juice
2 tablespoons grated onion, including juice
Dash of Worcestershire sauce
Salt and freshly ground black pepper to taste
Chopped parsley for garnish

Cocktail Complement:

Tequila Mockingbird
Margarita
(page 24)

1. Combine all ingredients but parsley in a food processor and pulse until smooth. Adjust seasoning to taste.
2. Transfer to a bowl and chill thoroughly. Top with chopped parsley.

Fresh-Cut Medley

Set the dip bowl in the middle of a platter and place a spoon in the dip. Garnish the platter with all or some of the following: fresh carrots, celery, cucumber, red peppers, zucchini, broccoli, cauliflower, green onions, pita triangles, toasted bread rounds, crackers, and breadsticks.

Stuffed Mediterranean Mushrooms

Cocktail Complement:

White Chocolatini
(page 14)

Serves 10

2/3 cup low-fat cottage cheese

3 ounces feta cheese, crumbled

2 tablespoons fresh snipped dill

1 teaspoon lemon juice

½ teaspoon olive oil

½ teaspoon dried oregano

Salt to taste

30 medium mushroom caps, cleaned and stemmed

Fresh dill sprigs for garnish

1. Combine the first seven ingredients in a small bowl and mix until blended thoroughly.
2. Spoon about 1 teaspoon of filling into each mushroom cap. Garnish with fresh dill sprigs and serve.

Poppin' Shrooms

Stuffed mushrooms are wonderful little appetizers that guests can pop in their mouths. Serve on an elegant tray of gold or silver. Some people do not like raw mushroom caps, so if you prefer, you can bake the mushroom caps for about 10 minutes. Just make sure that you allow them to cool before stuffing.

Cheese Party Ball

Serves 25

8 ounces cream cheese, softened
12 ounces blue cheese, crumbled
1 pound sharp cheddar cheese, shredded
1 tablespoon Worcestershire sauce
2 tablespoons onion, finely minced
Salt and white pepper to taste
1 cup pecans, toasted and roughly chopped

Cocktail
Complement:
Caramel Appletini
(page 18)

1. Using a wooden spoon or food processor, mix together all the ingredients, except the pecan chips, until smooth. Shape the mixture into 2 balls, about 1 pound each.
2. Roll each ball in the pecans to coat. Refrigerate immediately and serve chilled. The extra ball may be stored in the freezer, double wrapped in plastic film, for up to 1 month.

Just Say Cheese!

Why not serve this cheese ball at a wine and cheese party? Make invitations by writing with permanent marker on a wine glass—don't worry, it washes off of glass. Or mail out invitations on mousetraps, which you can find at the hardware store.

Fried Coconut Melon

Cocktail Complement:

Goin' Coconutini
(page 13)

Serves 4–5

2 pounds winter melon
7 tablespoons flour
½ cup flaked coconut
4 cups oil for deep-frying

1. Peel the winter melon and remove seeds. Cut into bite-sized pieces.
2. In a preheated wok or skillet, heat 4 cups of oil to 250°F. Just before frying, lightly dust a few melon pieces with flour. Slide those pieces into the wok. Deep-fry until light brown, being sure to keep the oil temperature around 250°F. Continue the process until all the melon is fried.
3. As you remove melon pieces from the wok, dust with the coconut and serve immediately.

Melon-choly Platter

Serve fried winter melon on a red platter decorated with chocolate watermelon seeds. To make the chocolate seeds, simply melt some chocolate in the microwave, dip your finger in the chocolate, and dot around the red or melon-colored platter to make it look like watermelon seeds. Arrange the Fried Coconut Melon on the platter.

Fried Bow Ties

Yields 2 bowties for every wrapper

1 package egg roll wrappers
¼ cup powdered sugar
Oil for deep-frying

Cocktail
Complement:
Wedding Reception
Bubbles
(page 101)

1. Cut each wrapper vertically into 4 equal pieces. Cut a 3/4-inch slit in the middle of each piece.
2. Take two long pieces and lay one piece on top of the other, then carefully tie a knot in the middle using both pieces. Your slits should end up in the knot. Starting with one side, tuck the two ends into the slit, then turn over and repeat with the other side. You should now have something that looks like a bow tie.
3. Heat 1½ inches of oil in a heavy skillet. Deep-fry a few of the bowties at a time until they are golden brown, turning over once. Remove from the pan with a slotted spoon and drain on paper towels.
4. Cool the bow ties and dust lightly with powdered sugar. Store in an airtight container. Serve cold.

Much-Kneaded Wrappers

If you prefer to make your own wrappers, here's a recipe. Homemade wrappers: 2 cups flour, 1 teaspoon salt, 1 egg, ½ cup ice water, cornstarch. Sift flour and salt into a bowl. Add egg and water. Stir until dough holds together. Turn out onto floured surface. Knead until smooth and elastic. Cover for 30 minutes. Divide dough and dust pastry board with cornstarch. Roll out. Cut into 3½- inch squares.

Fried Cauliflower

Cocktail Complement:

Come Hither
(page 90)

Serves 6

2 *heads cauliflower*
½ *bunch fresh parsley, chopped*
1 *whole egg*
2 *egg whites*
¼ *cup grated Parmesan cheese*
¼ *cup olive oil*
Fresh-cracked black pepper to taste

1. Cut the cauliflower into bite-size pieces. Chop the parsley.
2. Whisk the whole egg with the egg whites, then add the grated cheese and parsley.
3. Heat the oil to medium-high temperature in a large skillet. When the oil comes to temperature, dip the cauliflower in the egg mixture and drain off excess; place in the hot oil and fry on all sides until light golden brown. Drain on rack covered with paper towels. Season with pepper, and serve.

Flower Power

To add a colorful and yummy twist to this recipe, why not replace half of the cauliflower with broccoli to make fried cauliflower and fried broccoli? This dish would be great at a flower-power party!

Java Spice Snack Cake

Serves 16

1 cup honey

½ cup strong brewed coffee

1 tablespoon brandy

½ cup reduced-fat egg substitute

2 tablespoons olive oil

½ cup brown sugar, firmly packed

2 cups all-purpose flour

1½ teaspoons baking powder

1½ teaspoons baking soda

½ teaspoon salt

½ teaspoon ground cinnamon

¼ teaspoon ground ginger

1/8 teaspoon ground nutmeg

1/8 teaspoon ground cloves

Cocktail Complement:

Jack Be Nimble Java (page 76)

1. Preheat oven to 325°F. Add the honey, coffee, and brandy to a bowl and mix well. Add the egg substitute, oil, and brown sugar, and beat until combined.

2. Sift together the flour, baking powder, baking soda, salt, and spices, and fold into the mixture. Pour the batter into a 9" × 9" baking dish treated with nonstick cooking spray. Bake for 50 to 60 minutes, or until an inserted toothpick comes out clean. Slice into cubes.

Have Your Cake

Present the Java Spice Snack Cake on a pedestal cake stand with a shot glass of frilled toothpicks in the center. Guests can spear a cake cube at their convenience. If the cake stand doesn't hold all the cubes, simply place it on a platter and arrange the remaining cubes on the platter.

Spice-Up-Your-Life Popcorn

Cocktail Complement:

Super Bowl Drop Kick
(page 96)

Serves 2

4 cups low-fat microwave popcorn, popped
1 teaspoon Bragg's Liquid Aminos or low-sodium soy sauce
2 teaspoons fresh lemon juice
1 teaspoon five-spice powder
¼ teaspoon ground coriander
¼ teaspoon garlic powder

1. Preheat oven to 250°F. Spread the popcorn on a nonstick cookie sheet and lightly coat with nonstick or butter-flavored cooking spray.
2. Mix together all the remaining ingredients. Drizzle the mixture over the popcorn and lightly toss to coat evenly. Bake for 5 minutes, toss the popcorn and rotate the pan, and then bake for an additional 5 minutes. Serve warm.

Spicy Popcorn

Double, triple, or quadruple the recipe to make popcorn for many. Serve in bowls around the room if you are hosting a party for a television event, such as the Super Bowl.

Get Your Snack Mixer On

Serves 16

6 cups mixed cereal
*   (such as unsweetened bran, oat, rice,*
*   and wheat cereal mix)*
1 cup mini bow-knot pretzels
2/3 cup dry-roasted peanuts
1/8 cup (2 tablespoons) butter, melted
1/8 cup (2 tablespoons) olive, canola, or peanut oil
1 tablespoon Worcestershire sauce
¼ teaspoon garlic powder
Tabasco sauce or other liquid hot pepper sauce, to taste

Cocktail Complement:

Lucky Charmartini
(page 17)

1. Preheat oven to 300°F. In a large bowl, combine the cereal, pretzels, and peanuts. In another bowl, combine the butter, oil, Worcestershire, garlic powder, and Tabasco (if using).
2. Pour liquid ingredients over the cereal mixture and toss to coat evenly. Spread the mixture on a large baking sheet and bake for 30 to 40 minutes, stirring every 10 minutes, until crisp and dry.

Mingling Mixer

Present the snack mix in bowls set around the room to encourage munching. This is also a great first-round appetizer—early guests can nibble on it while you finish up the real treats that you are preparing for your party. Extra snack mix can be stored in airtight plastic bags until needed again.

Smoked Mussel Spread

Cocktail Complement:

Death by Chocolatini
(page 20)

Yields 4¼ cups

4 ounces cream cheese

1 cup nonfat plain yogurt

½ cup nonfat cottage cheese

2 ounces Ducktrap River smoked mussels

¼ cup chopped onion or scallion

1 teaspoon dried dill

1 teaspoon dried parsley

Place all the ingredients in a food processor or blender and process until smooth. Chill for at least 2 hours or overnight before serving.

Spread Out

This Smoked Mussel Spread also works well made with smoked oysters, smoked shrimp, or smoked turkey. Present the spread in a bowl in the middle of a silver, gold, black, or white platter. Arrange assorted crackers or cracker-sized bread rounds around the bowl. A side bowl of pitted black olives would make a nice addition.

French Skinny Dip

Yields about 1¾ cups

1 cup chopped sweet onion
1 tablespoon Parmesan cheese
1 cup nonfat cottage cheese
1 tablespoon reduced (double-strength) beef broth

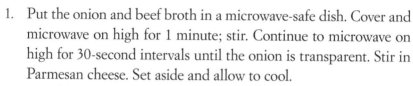

Cocktail
Complement:

Ain't Misbehavin'
Mary
(page 139)

1. Put the onion and beef broth in a microwave-safe dish. Cover and microwave on high for 1 minute; stir. Continue to microwave on high for 30-second intervals until the onion is transparent. Stir in Parmesan cheese. Set aside and allow to cool.
2. In a blender, process the cottage cheese until smooth. Mix the cottage cheese into the onion mixture. Serve warm, or refrigerate until needed and serve cold.

Calling All Dippers

French Skinny Dip can be presented in a bowl in the middle of a platter surrounded by dippers. Your options for dippers are endless. Here are some to get you started: carrot sticks, celery, cucumber rounds, red, yellow, and green pepper strips, zucchini rounds or sticks, broccoli and cauliflower pieces, green onions, pita triangles, toasted bread rounds, crackers, and breadsticks.

Spicy Almond Dip

Yields about ½ cup

¼ cup ground raw almonds
2 teaspoons Worcestershire sauce
½ teaspoon honey
½ teaspoon chili powder
1 teaspoon poppy seeds
½ teaspoon onion powder
1/8 cup water
Pinch of black pepper

Put all the ingredients in a food processor and blend until smooth.

Cocktail
Complement:

Almond Joytini
(page 20)

Get Sauced

Worcestershire sauce is a spicy sauce composed mainly of water, vinegar, molasses, corn syrup, anchovies, spices, and flavorings. It's a great flavor for sauces, dips, and Bloody Marys, and it's good for marinating meats. It should be used sparingly, as it has a very strong flavor. A good brand to try is Lea & Perrins.

Smoked Salmon Cucumber

Cocktail Complement:

Cool as a Cucumber (page 137)

Yields about ½ cup

2–3 cucumbers
1 ounce smoked salmon
8 ounces Neufchatel cheese, room temperature
½ tablespoon lemon juice
½ teaspoon freshly ground pepper
Dried dill (optional)

1. Cut the cucumbers into slices about ¼-inch thick. Place the slices on paper towels to drain while you prepare the salmon cream.
2. Combine the smoked salmon, Neufchatel cheese, lemon juice, and pepper in a food processor; blend until smooth.
3. Fit a pastry bag with your choice of tip, and spoon the salmon cream into the bag. Pipe 1 teaspoon of the salmon cream atop each cucumber slice. Garnish with dried dill, if desired.

Soft Cheese

Neufchatel cheese originated in Normandy, France. It's a very soft, spreadable cheese similar to cream cheese that is made from whole milk rather than cream. It is sold molded into many shapes, traditionally a heart. However, in North America it is more commonly found in a brick form.

chapter 14

Hors d'Oeuvres

Miso Mad for Avocado

Cocktail Complement:

Mango Virgo
(page 137)

Serves 2

1 ripe Haas avocado, halved, seeded, and peeled
1 lemon
1 teaspoon white or yellow miso
1 teaspoon grated ginger root
1 teaspoon light soy sauce
1 teaspoon sugar
1 teaspoon sesame oil
Wasabi paste for garnish
Pickled ginger for garnish

1. Place the avocado halves on a board, cut side down; slice them at 1/8-inch intervals, leaving the stem end connected to hold slices together. Squeeze the lemon over the scored avocados to prevent browning. Fan the avocados onto 2 small plates.
2. Whisk together the miso, ginger, soy sauce, sugar, and sesame oil until the sugar is dissolved. Spoon some of the dressing over the avocadoes. Serve garnished with wasabi and pickled ginger.

Avocado Fan

For a larger guest list, fan out four avocados in a circle on a larger plate. The colors will be avocado green from the avocados and dark brown from the dressing, so make sure that you use a light-colored plate to pop the presentation. Also, if you desire, squeeze some lemon juice on the avocado to prevent browning.

Fried Stoplight Tomatoes

Serves 4

1 cup mayonnaise

1 hard-boiled egg, finely chopped

1 tablespoon capers, chopped

1 tablespoon chopped dill pickle

1 teaspoon chopped parsley

Dash of hot pepper sauce or cayenne

1 large green tomato, sliced ½-inch thick

1 large firm yellow tomato, sliced ½-inch thick

1 large firm red tomato, sliced ½-inch thick

Flour for dredging

6 eggs, beaten, diluted with ½ cup milk

4 cups plain or seasoned bread crumbs, preferably homemade

3 cups light oil, such as canola or peanut, for frying

Cocktail Complement:

Road Rage at the Traffic Light (page 50)

1. Make the remoulade sauce: Combine mayonnaise with chopped egg, capers, pickle, parsley, and hot sauce. Season to taste, and refrigerate.

2. Dredge each tomato slice in flour, then eggs, then bread crumbs, pressing the bread crumbs to ensure adherence. Fry in small batches over low-medium heat (325°F oil temperature), until they feel tender when tested with a fork. Season with salt, and serve immediately with remoulade sauce.

Toe May Toe; Toe Mah Toe

Fan the fried tomatoes around a plate and set the sauce in the middle. Since the coloring of the fried tomatoes and sauce will be natural, try to use a bright-colored plate like red, yellow, or green. Another option is to arrange the tomatoes on red or green curly leaf lettuce.

Corny Tofu Tortilla Wraps

Cocktail Complement:

Muy Bonita Rita (page 30)

Serves 4

½ cup wheat berries, spelt, taro,
  or other whole grain
2 ears corn, kernels sheared from the cob
  and boiled 1 minute, or
  1 10-ounce package frozen sweet corn, thawed
Juice of 1 lemon
1 tablespoon extra-virgin olive oil
½ teaspoon ground cumin
Salt and pepper to taste
2 tablespoons salad dressing (such as Miracle Whip)
4 medium flour tortillas (10–12 inches)
1 cup flavored tofu (such as spicy or Asian flavors)

1. Boil the grain until tender (usually about 30 minutes).
2. In a bowl, toss the cooked grain, corn, lemon juice, olive oil, salt, and pepper until combined.
3. Spread the dressing in a line across the middle of each tortilla. Spoon in the grain salad; arrange the tofu alongside the grain.
4. Roll, jelly-roll style, away from yourself. Tuck in ends.

Wrapping It Up

Arrange the rolled tortilla wraps on a bed of lettuce in an interesting way. Or cut the rolls in half and present them vertically, cut side up, in colorful cups or bowls. Make sure at least half of the roll is left sticking up and out for easy picking. Great for a Cinco de Mayo party!

Wrapping to the Beet

Serves 4

4 flour tortillas (10-inch diameter or larger)
2 tablespoons mayonnaise or sour cream
2 cups succotash salad (recipe follows)
1 large or 2 small beets (about 8 ounces), boiled until tender, peeled
1 ripe Florida avocado, peeled, cut into 1-inch wedges
Kosher salt

Cocktail Complement:

Earth Angel Sangria (page 141)

1. Soften and lightly brown the tortillas by placing them directly on the burner of a gas or electric range until surface blisters slightly, flipping frequently. (Alternately, steam, broil, or toast them for a minute until soft.)

2. Spread ½ tablespoon of mayonnaise into a line across the center of each tortilla. Spoon ½ cup of succotash onto each tortilla. Halve the beets and cut the halves into ½-inch slices. Divide the beets and avocado slices evenly onto the tortillas, placing them on the side of the succotash line closest to you.

3. Place 1 of the tortillas on a work surface directly in front of you. Fold the near edge of the tortilla over the fillings, and roll it, jellyroll fashion, away from yourself, keeping even pressure to ensure a tight roll.

Sucker for Succotash

To make your own succotash salad, mix ½ cup lima beans, ½ cup corn, ½ cup diced green beans, ½ cup diced plum tomatoes, and a little diced onion with 1/8 cup olive oil, 1/8 cup cider vinegar, ½ teaspoon Dijon mustard, a pinch of sugar, and salt and pepper to taste. Add chopped garlic if you desire.

She Rolls Sushi by the Seashore

Cocktail Complement:

White Sangria (page 112)

Yields 6 rolls

4½ cups sushi rice

7 sheets nori

6 cooked, peeled, and chilled shrimp

1 cup cucumber, cut in fine julienne

1 ripe Haas avocado, cut into thin strips, sprinkled with lemon juice and salt

1 cup store-bought marinated tofu or flavored tempeh, cut into small strips

2 teaspoons wasabi

1. Place one sheet of nori on a sushi-rolling mat with the long edge toward you. Spread about 3/4 cup rice onto the nori, leaving a 1-inch strip free at the far end. Use your hands, moistened with water, to smooth the rice into an even layer.

2. On the edge closest to you, spread a thin line of wasabi. Arrange a sixth of the cucumber, a sixth of the avocado, one shrimp cut in half, and a sixth of the tofu or tempeh into a strip near the wasabi-laced edge. Using the mat as a helper, roll the assembly jelly-roll style away from yourself. Keep pressure even and firm, and keep the mat clear of the roll.

3. Repeat the procedure with remaining nori and fillings. Allow to stand for 5 minutes before slicing each roll into 6 pieces. Serve with wasabi and pickled ginger.

All-Purpose Asian Dipping Sauce

For anything from crisp fried snacks (like spring rolls, tempura, and chips) to hot dim sum dumplings or chilled vegetables, an easy dipping sauce can be whipped up in a minute by combining equal amounts of soy sauce and rice vinegar, and sprinkling in a few drops of Asian sesame oil. For extra flavor, add chopped or julienned fresh ginger and/or a few sesame seeds.

Wild Mushroom Huff-n-Puffs

Cocktail
Complement:

Eternal Flame
(page 68)

Yields 24 pieces

24 pieces frozen puff pastry hors d'oeuvre shells
1 tablespoon unsalted butter
2 cups (about ½ pound) assorted wild mushrooms,
*   such as morels, chanterelles, oysters, shiitakes,*
*   and/or domestic and cremini mushrooms*
½ teaspoon salt
2 sprigs fresh rosemary, leaves picked and chopped
¼ cup vegetable stock or water
1 teaspoon cornstarch dissolved in 1 tablespoon cold water
Freshly ground black pepper to taste
Squeeze of lemon

1. Bake puff pastry shells according to package directions and set aside.
2. Melt the butter in a medium skillet over medium heat. Add the mushrooms and cook without stirring for 5 minutes, until nicely browned. Add salt and rosemary; cook 3 minutes more. Add the stock and cornstarch; stir until thickened and bubbling. Remove from heat; adjust seasoning with black pepper, a few drops of lemon, and salt to taste.
3. Spoon ½ teaspoon of mushroom mixture into each shell. Serve piping hot.

Get Puffed

The bite-sized puff pastry shells are extremely inviting and can be presented simply on a silver platter. Party stores sell inexpensive silver and gold plastic platters in all shapes and sizes that work well. The best thing is that they can be used again and again. To dress them up even more, try using doilies.

Fried Green Tomato Bruschetta

Serves 4

4 medium green tomatoes, sliced ½-inch thick

Flour for dredging

2 eggs, beaten

1 cup plain bread crumbs

Oil for frying (preferably olive oil)

1 tablespoon balsamic vinegar

¼ cup chopped fresh basil leaves (plus a few whole leaves for garnish)

12 green olives with pimiento, halved lengthwise

¼ cup extra-virgin olive oil

1 loaf crusty country bread, sliced 1-inch thick

Cocktail Complement:

Itsy Bitsy Teenie Weenie Yellow Polka Dot Martini (page 12)

1. Dredge tomato slices in flour. Dip in egg and then in breadcrumbs, shaking off excess after each dip. Fry at low heat (about 325°F) until golden and mostly tender (a little underdone is good). Place the still-hot tomatoes flat on a cutting board and dice them into ½-inch pieces.
2. In a large mixing bowl, gently toss the diced tomatoes with the vinegar, basil, and olives. Set aside.
3. Brush the bread slices with extra-virgin oil, and grill or oven-toast at 400°F until lightly browned. This can also be done under the broiler. Top each slice with tomato mixture. Cut in half, and serve garnished with a small basil sprig.

The Country of Italy

This bruschetta is down-home country meets Italy, so you can present it many ways. For a down-home country feel as well as an Italian feel, try arranging the bruschetta on a red-and-white gingham–covered platter. You might also serve on a clean washboard or in clean black cast-iron skillet.

Heavenly Half-Moons

Yields about 30 pieces

2 cups dried pitted prunes
½ cup pineapple juice
1 tablespoon grated orange zest
¼ cup granulated sugar
¼ cup shredded coconut
¼ cup walnuts, finely chopped
Wonton wraps
Oil for deep-frying
1 egg white, lightly beaten
Powdered sugar

Cocktail Complement:

Hot Buttered Sugarplum Rum

(page 80)

1. Make the filling: In a saucepan, combine the prunes, pineapple juice, orange zest, and sugar. Place over moderately low heat, bring to a simmer, and cook until reduced to the consistency of a paste. Remove from heat and cool. Stir in coconut and walnuts.
2. Place the wonton wraps on a flat surface. Using a cookie cutter, cut the largest possible circle out of each wonton wrapper; discard scraps.
3. Brush the edges of a circle with the egg white. (You can do 2 or 3 at a time, but no more—otherwise the wraps will stick to your work surface.) Place ½ teaspoon of filling in the center of each circle. Fold over to form a half moon. Press firmly to seal the edges. Place on a lightly oiled baking sheet.
4. In a large saucepan or a deep fryer, pour in oil to a depth of 2 inches and heat to 375°F on a deep-fat thermometer. Fry the half-moons, 8 at a time, turning once, until golden brown on both sides. Using a slotted spoon, remove and let drain on paper towels. Arrange on a platter and sprinkle with the powdered sugar.

Fried Spaghetti

Cocktail
Complement:

Bloody Mary
(page 112)

Serves 4

12 ounces spaghetti
4 tablespoons unsalted butter
3 eggs
1/3 cup milk
½ cup freshly grated Parmesan cheese, plus additional for serving
2 tablespoons fresh parsley, finely chopped
2 tablespoons scallions, finely chopped
Salt and freshly ground black pepper to taste

1. In a large pot, bring at least 4 quarts of water to a rolling boil. Add 1 tablespoon salt. Add the spaghetti and stir to separate strands. Cook until not quite al dente. Drain. Transfer to a warm bowl and toss with 1 tablespoon of the butter. Cool to room temperature.
2. Beat together the eggs and milk with an electric mixer. Beat in the Parmesan. Stir in the parsley and scallions. Add salt and fresh pepper to taste. Pour the egg mixture over the pasta and toss well.
3. Melt the remaining 3 tablespoons of butter in a large skillet. When the butter foams, turn spaghetti mixture into the skillet. Spread and flatten the pasta into a pancake and cook over low heat until a golden crust forms on the bottom. Invert onto a plate, flip over, and cook other side to form another crust.
4. Slide the pancake out onto a hot plate and sprinkle with additional grated cheese to taste. Cut into wedges and serve hot or warm.

Spaghetti Wedges

Layer the fried spaghetti wedges point side out in a circle, as if you are building a Christmas tree from the ground up. This will keep the wedges of fried spaghetti warmer longer and create a nice presentation. Serve additional Parmesan cheese in a bowl on the side if desired.

Roasted and Toasted Ravioli

Yields about 40 pieces

Ravioli

1-pound bag small cheese ravioli
1 tablespoon plus ½ teaspoon salt
½ cup heavy cream
1 tablespoon beaten egg
3/4 cup dry plain bread crumbs
1 tablespoon finely chopped
    fresh parsley
½ teaspoon garlic powder
Vegetable oil for frying
5 tablespoons butter, melted
½ cup freshly grated Parmesan cheese

Cocktail Complement:

Lemon Love Shack Shake (page 93)

Pesto Cream Sauce

¼ cup store-bought pesto
1 cup heavy cream
1 tablespoon unsalted butter
1/3 cup freshly grated
    Parmesan cheese

1. In a large pot, bring at least 4 quarts of water to a rolling boil. Add the tablespoon of salt. Add the ravioli and stir to prevent sticking. Cook until al dente. Drain, pat dry, and let cool.
2. In a shallow bowl, mix together cream and beaten egg.
3. In a medium bowl, combine bread crumbs, parsley, the ½ teaspoon salt, and garlic powder.
4. Dip each ravioli in the cream and egg mixture, then coat well with the bread crumb mixture. Set on a baking sheet lined with waxed paper.
5. In a large, heavy skillet, heat about ½ inch of oil until hot, about 375°F. In small batches, fry the ravioli until golden, about 30 seconds. Place on paper towels to drain.
6. Before serving, arrange the ravioli in a baking dish. Drizzle with the melted butter and sprinkle with the Parmesan. Bake in a preheated 350°F oven until hot and puffy, about 10 minutes.
7. Make the sauce: Combine the pesto, cream, and butter in a saucepan and bring to a simmer over low heat. Let simmer slowly for about 5 minutes. Before serving, slowly stir in the grated Parmesan. Place sauce in a small serving bowl alongside the ravioli.

Dunkin' Dumplings

Yields 15–20 dumplings

¼ cup sticky rice flour

1 cup rice flour

½ cup water

¼ cup tapioca flour

1 teaspoon vegetable oil

2 cups chives, cut into ½-inch lengths

1 tablespoon soy sauce

Cocktail Complement:

Goldilocks Platinum Blonde Coffee (page 73)

1. In a medium-sized saucepan, stir together the sticky rice flour and the rice flour. Add the water and stir thoroughly to blend. Turn the heat to medium and cook, stirring constantly until the mixture has the consistency of glue. (If the mixture becomes too sticky, reduce the heat to low.) Remove the batter from the heat and quickly stir in the tapioca flour. Set aside to cool to room temperature.

2. Meanwhile, add the vegetable oil to a skillet large enough to easily hold the chives, and heat on high. Add the chives and the soy sauce. Stir-fry the chives just until they wilt. Be careful not to let the chives cook too much. Remove from heat and set aside.

3. Once the dough has reached room temperature, check its consistency. If it is too sticky to work with, add a bit more tapioca flour.

4. To make the dumplings, roll the batter into balls 1 inch in diameter. Using your fingers, flatten each ball into a disk about 4 inches across. Spoon about 1 tablespoon of the chives into the middle of each disk. Fold the disk in half and pinch the edges together to form a half-moon–shaped packet. Place the dumplings in a prepared steamer for 5 to 8 minutes or until the dough is cooked. Serve with a spicy dipping sauce of your choice.

Italian Steering Wheels

Cocktail
Complement:
Sangria
(page 113)

Makes 24 pieces

Filling

1½ pounds whole-milk ricotta cheese

3 cloves garlic, minced

4 ounces pecorino Romano cheese,
    freshly grated

½ cup Parmesan cheese, freshly grated

½ cup oil-packed sun-dried tomatoes,
    coarsely chopped

½ cup toasted walnuts, coarsely chopped

2 tablespoons finely chopped parsley

1/3 cup scallions, finely chopped

½ teaspoon dried hot red pepper flakes

¼ teaspoon white ground pepper

Salt to taste

Pasta

1 tablespoon salt

12 ruffle-edged lasagna noodles

1. Make the filling: In a large bowl, combine all the filling ingredients and mix very well, adjusting the salt to taste.
2. Meanwhile, prepare the pasta: In a large pot, bring at least 4 quarts of water to a rolling boil. Add the tablespoon salt. Add the lasagna noodles, stirring carefully. Cook until al dente. To drain, do not pour the noodles directly into a colander or they will stick together. Bring the pot to the sink and position over a colander. Run cold water into the pot as you pour out the hot. Let noodles fall into colander. Grab each one with your hand. Gently shake, and place on a paper towel or cloth to blot. Keep moist under a lightly dampened towel until ready to fill.
3. To fill: Take 1 lasagna noodle and spread with about ½ cup of the filling. Roll each noodle up lengthwise into a tight roll. Cut each horizontally in half. Place, cut side down, on a lightly greased baking sheet.
4. When ready to serve, bake in a preheated 350°F oven until warm, about 10 minutes. Do not overbake.

Fried Wontons

Cocktail Complement:

Papa Bear's
Black Honey
(page 74)

Yields approximately 25 wontons

1 clove garlic, minced
2 tablespoons minced cilantro
2 tablespoons soy sauce
½ cup white mushrooms, chopped
Pinch white pepper
½ pound ground pork
25 wonton skins
Vegetable oil for frying

1. In a medium-sized mixing bowl, thoroughly combine the garlic, cilantro, soy sauce, mushrooms, white pepper, and ground pork.
2. To make the wontons, place approximately ½ teaspoon of the filling in the middle of a wonton skin. Fold the wonton from corner to corner, forming a triangle. Press the edges together to seal closed. Repeat with the remaining skins and filling.
3. Add about 2 to 3 inches of vegetable oil to a deep fryer or wok. Heat the oil on medium until it reaches about 350°F. Carefully add the wontons, 2 or 3 at a time. Fry until they are golden brown, turning them constantly. Transfer the cooked wontons to drain on paper towels as they are done.
4. Serve the wontons with either sweet-and-sour sauce or the sauce of your choice.

Golden Wontons

The fried wontons will be a golden color when finished, so stay away from beige and tan serving dishes. Use bright colors to pop the wonton in your display or shiny chrome or gold tone with crisp white doilies. Scout your local thrift store for clever displays to present your wontons.

Shrimp Boat Toasts

Cocktail Complement:

Lemondrop
(page 123)

Yields 48 pieces

1 pound peeled cooked shrimp
¼ cup minced green onions
2 tablespoons minced fresh cilantro
1 teaspoon minced garlic
1 teaspoon minced jalapeño pepper
1 large egg white
1 tablespoon nonfat dry milk
4 ounces cream cheese, cut into pieces
½ cup plain nonfat yogurt
12 (1-ounce) slices white bread, crusts removed
Spectrum Naturals Extra Virgin Olive Spray Oil with Garlic Flavor
Spectrum Naturals Canola Spray Oil with Butter Flavor

1. Preheat oven to 375°F.
2. In a food processor, combine the shrimp, green onions, cilantro, garlic, jalapeño, egg white, and nonfat dry milk; process until smooth. Add cubes of cream cheese and pulse to incorporate. Add the yogurt and pulse just until incorporated, being careful not to overprocess.
3. Toast bread (to shorten the baking time and help keep it crisp in the center). Lightly spray bottom of each slice with the garlic-flavored oil. Evenly divide the shrimp mixture among the slices of bread, spreading it on the nonsprayed side of the bread and making sure to spread it to the edges of the bread.
4. Place the coated bread slices (shrimp mixture–side up) on a baking sheet treated with nonstick spray or covered with nonstick foil. Lightly spray the tops of the bread with the butter-flavored spray oil. Bake for 10 to 15 minutes, or until the bread is crisp and the shrimp topping bubbles and is lightly browned. Use a pizza cutter or serrated knife to cut each slice of bread into 4 equal pieces. Arrange on a tray or platter and serve immediately.

Ginger and Mary Ann Clams

Cocktail
Complement:

Long Island Tea
(page 123)

Serves 2

2 teaspoons Bragg's Liquid Aminos or
    low-sodium soy sauce
1 teaspoon lemon juice
¼ cup spring onions, thinly sliced
1 teaspoon white rice-wine vinegar
4 teaspoons apple juice
1 teaspoon ground ginger
¼ teaspoon Oriental mustard powder
4 cloves garlic, minced, or 1 teaspoon garlic powder
1 teaspoon dried green onion flakes
¼ teaspoon granulated sugar
1 15-ounce can Gordon's Chesapeake Classics
    Cocktail Clams (steamer size), drained
1 large cucumber

1. In a bowl, combine all ingredients except the steamer clams and cucumber. Add the drained clams and toss to mix.
2. Wash and slice the cucumber. Arrange the cucumber slices on a platter and place a clam atop each slice. Chill until ready to serve.

Surf's Up!

Here's another great dish for a nautical-themed party. Try arranging the clams on a clean boogie or surfboard to make your guests' eyes light up. Drape clean netting over the middle of the board and place the Ginger and Mary Ann clams on top. Decorate with little white lights and seashells.

Dandy Brandy Swiss Fondue

Cocktail Complement:
Autumn in New York
(page 103)

Serves 2

1 garlic clove

1 tablespoon flour

½ cup vegetable broth

1/3 cup evaporated milk

¼ teaspoon brandy or brandy-flavored extract

1 tablespoon fresh Parmesan cheese

2 ounces (¼ cup) Swiss cheese

2 ounces (¼ cup) cream cheese

1/8 teaspoon black pepper, freshly ground

1/8 teaspoon ground nutmeg

1 loaf French bread, cubed

1. Peel the garlic and cut in half lengthwise. Rub the inside of the slow cooker with the cut sides of the garlic. Discard the garlic. Whisk the flour and 1 tablespoon of the vegetable broth in a measuring cup until well blended. Add the remaining broth and the milk to the slow cooker and cook, uncovered, on high setting. Whisk in the brandy and the flour mixture. Cook, stirring constantly, for about 5 minutes.

2. Shred the Parmesan and Swiss cheeses using a vegetable or cheese grater. Cut the cream cheese into 1-inch cubes. Add the Parmesan cheese, Swiss cheese, cream cheese, pepper, and nutmeg to the slow cooker. Cook on high setting, stirring constantly until the cheeses melt and the mixture is very smooth.

3. Turn the slow cooker to the low setting for serving. Serve from the slow cooker to keep the fondue from solidifying. Use fondue forks or bamboo skewers to dip the bread.

Mardi Gras Cabbage Patch Rolls

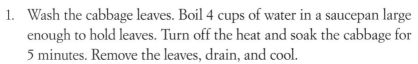

Cocktail Complement:

Ragin' Cajun
Mardi Gras Punch
(page 97)

Serves 12

12 large cabbage leaves (6 purple, 6 green)
1 pound lean ground beef
½ cup cooked white rice
½ teaspoon salt
1/8 teaspoon ground black pepper
¼ teaspoon thyme
¼ teaspoon nutmeg
¼ teaspoon cinnamon
1 6-ounce can tomato paste
3/4 cup water

1. Wash the cabbage leaves. Boil 4 cups of water in a saucepan large enough to hold leaves. Turn off the heat and soak the cabbage for 5 minutes. Remove the leaves, drain, and cool.
2. Combine the ground beef, rice, salt, pepper, thyme, nutmeg, and cinnamon. Place 2 tablespoons of the meat mixture on each leaf and roll firmly. Stack the cabbage rolls in the slow cooker. Combine the tomato paste and water; pour over the stuffed cabbage rolls. Cook covered on low setting 8 to 9 hours.

Fat Tuesday

Try this dish at a Mardi Gras party! Cover the bottom of a chafing dish with dark green lettuce and sliced yellow peppers. Then place the cabbage rolls on top. Buy inexpensive hurricane plastic glasses at a party store and tie a ribbon around with an invitation attached. Decorate with purple, green, and gold!

Porcupine Meatballs

Cocktail Complement:

Latitude Attitude
Adjuster
(page 40)

Serves 6

½ cup chopped yellow onion

½ cup chopped green bell pepper

1½ cups lean ground beef

½ cup uncooked white rice

1 egg

1 teaspoon table salt

½ teaspoon ground black pepper

1 (103/4-ounce) can condensed tomato soup

1. Peel and chop the onion into 1/8-inch pieces. Remove the stem and seeds from the green pepper and chop into 1/8-inch pieces. In a mixing bowl, combine the ground beef, rice, onion, green pepper, egg, salt, and pepper. Mix well with your hands until blended.

2. Shape the mixture into about 24 golf ball–sized meatballs. Place in the slow cooker. Pour the soup over the meatballs. Cover and cook on low setting for 7 to 8 hours.

Bamboo Meatballs

You can always keep the meatballs in the slow cooker with the heat set on low and bamboo skewers on the side for serving. Or take them out and serve in a chafing dish with round toothpicks for spearing. Make sure that you provide your guests with napkins near this dish. This is a great dish to serve at a luau or barbeque!

Portobello-Stuffed Artichokes

Cocktail
Complement:
Pink Cadillactini
(page 15)

Serves 4

4 large artichokes
4 large portobello mushrooms
3 garlic cloves
2 tablespoons grated Parmesan cheese
½ teaspoon ground black pepper
1 tablespoon olive oil
1 teaspoon salt

1. Remove the stems from the artichokes and discard the outer 2 or 3 layers of leaves. Trim the base so that the artichokes stand flat. Cut off the top of the artichoke and hollow out the center, removing all purple-tinged leaves and fuzzy material.
2. Chop the mushrooms into ¼-inch pieces. Peel the garlic and mince. Combine the mushrooms, garlic, Parmesan cheese, black pepper, and olive oil in a medium-sized mixing bowl. Stuff the mixture into the artichoke centers.
3. Pour water into the slow cooker to a depth of about 1½ inches. Stir in the salt. Set the artichokes in the water. Cover and cook on low setting for 7 to 9 hours. The leaves should be tender when done. To eat, first use the artichoke leaves to scoop up some portobello stuffing, then use your teeth to scrape the artichoke and stuffing straight into your mouth.

Petal Strip

Most people do not know how to eat an artichoke. You simply enjoy a leaf at a time by pulling the base of the leaf through slightly clenched teeth to strip off the meat of the artichoke. You then discard the leaf.

Strawberry Brie Chutney

Cocktail
Complement:

Strawberry Mojitorita
(page 24)

Serves 8–12

1 cup strawberries

½ cup brown sugar

1/3 cup cider vinegar

1/8 teaspoon nutmeg

2 tablespoons grapefruit juice

1 8-ounce piece of Brie cheese

1 tablespoon sliced almonds, toasted

1. Remove the green tops from the strawberries and slice berries in quarters. Combine the strawberries, brown, sugar, vinegar, nutmeg, and grapefruit juice in slow cooker. Cover and cook on low setting for 4 hours. Remove top, turn heat to high, and cook 30 minutes, stirring every few minutes. Put mixture in refrigerator to cool.
2. Preheat oven to 350°F.
3. Place the Brie on an ovenproof plate and cover with sliced almonds; bake uncovered in oven for about 10 minutes. Cheese should be partially melted but not fully melted. Remove from the oven and top with room-temperature chutney.

Free Brie

This treat is fantastic for a wine and cheese party! Cut the brie so that your guests don't have to spend time cutting it themselves. Also, don't try to get fancy by placing the Brie on top of a bed of ruffled lettuce, because it will be hard to serve. Make sure that you provide small dishes and forks aside this dish as well.

Stuffed Sweet Peppers

Cocktail
Complement:

Tom Collins
(page 129)

Serves 6

12–18 large fresh peppers
   (sweet Italian variety, such as banana peppers)
2 garlic cloves
1 small white onion
1 large ripe tomato
1 teaspoon capers
¼ cup chopped green olives
1 tablespoon candied lemon peel
¼ cup almonds
2 eggs
4 whole cloves
5 peppercorns
½ pound ham
3 tablespoons shortening
1 pound lean ground pork
2 tablespoons snipped parsley
3 tablespoons cider vinegar
½ teaspoon vanilla extract
2 tablespoons granulated sugar
¼ teaspoon ground nutmeg
1/8 teaspoon powdered saffron
¼ cup seedless raisins
½ cup flour
1 cup vegetable oil

1. Cut out the stems of the peppers, leaving the peppers whole.
   Scoop out the seeds and membrane. Place the peppers in a large
   saucepan. Cover with boiling water, bring to a boil, and cook for
   about 2 minutes. Drain and invert the peppers on a paper towel.
2. Peel and mince the garlic. Peel the onion and chop into ¼-inch
   pieces. Remove the stem from the tomato and chop into ¼-inch

pieces. Mince the capers and finely chop the green olives, lemon peel, and almonds. Beat the eggs and set aside. Crush the cloves and peppercorns. Grind the ham using a meat grinder.

3. Heat the shortening in a large frying pan. Add the garlic, onion, and both meats. Cook until the meat is browned, stirring occasionally.

4. Mix together the tomatoes, parsley, vinegar, vanilla extract, sugar, cloves, peppercorns, nutmeg, and saffron; add mixture to the meat along with almonds, raisins, capers, lemon peel, and olives. Stir. Cook over low heat, stirring frequently, until the mixture is almost dry, about 30 to 40 minutes. Spoon the filling into the peppers, packing tightly so the mixture will remain in the pepper cavities during frying.

5. Roll the peppers in the flour, coating entire surface. Dip in the beaten eggs.

6. Heat the oil to medium-high in a large frying pan. Fry peppers until golden. Place on paper towels to drain off grease.

Festive Peppers

Present the fried peppers on a bed of curly red or green leaf lettuce. For a festive presentation, find a ceramic chip and dip sombrero and arrange the stuffed peppers around the rim of the sombrero. Fill the dip container with marinara sauce, or just fill up the cavity with more stuffed peppers.

Hawaiian Honey Wings

Cocktail Complement:

Hawaiian Luau
Jungle Juice
(page 102)

Serves 12

3 pounds chicken wings
1 garlic clove
1 cup cubed pineapple, fresh or canned
½ teaspoon salt
½ teaspoon ground black pepper
1 cup honey
½ cup soy sauce
2 tablespoons vegetable oil

1. Cut the tip off each chicken wing and discard. Mince the garlic with a sharp kitchen knife. Cut the pineapple into 1-inch cubes.
2. Combine the pineapple with salt, pepper, honey, soy sauce, vegetable oil, and garlic in a bowl. Mix well. Place the wings in the slow cooker. Pour the sauce over the wings and cook, covered, on low setting for 6 to 7 hours.

Fly to Hawaii

These wings will give flight to your Hawaiian luau! Serve the wings in Crock-Pot set on low. Tie a grass skirt from the party store around the top off the slow cooker. Allow the skirt to fan on the table. Set small plates and napkins on the skirt so that guests can easily serve themselves without any trouble.

Brie and Papaya Quesadillas

Cocktail
Complement:
White Sangriarita
(page 25)

Yields 36 wedges

½ medium-sized yellow onion
2 large red chili peppers
1 ripe papaya
1 pound brie
½ cup water
12 flour tortillas
4 tablespoons butter
4 tablespoons oil

1. Remove the peel from the onion and cut into ¼-inch-thick slices. Remove the stems from the chili peppers and dice into pieces about 1/8-inch square. Peel and seed the papaya; dice into pieces about 1/8-inch square. Cut the brie into ¼-inch strips.
2. Heat the water on high in a medium-sized skillet until boiling. Remove from heat and add the onions; let stand for 10 to 15 minutes. Drain and set aside.
3. Preheat oven to 250°F. Warm the tortillas by placing them in the oven for 10 minutes. Melt the butter in a small saucepan over low heat. Add the oil to the butter and stir until mixed. Remove the tortillas from the oven but leave the oven at 250°F.
4. Place a few strips of cheese on each tortilla. Add several onion strips, ½ teaspoon of diced chili peppers, and 1 tablespoon of diced papaya. Add another tortilla to make a sandwich, then brush the top tortilla with the butter and oil mixture.
5. Place the quesadillas one at a time in a large skillet on medium heat. Brown both sides. Place the quesadillas on a baking sheet in the oven to keep warm while the others are being made. Cut each quesadilla into 6 triangular wedges to serve.

Lollipop Chicken

Cocktail Complement:

Charming Proposal
(page 91)

Serves 4

2 tablespoons ginger garlic paste

4 tablespoons all-purpose flour

4 tablespoons corn flour

3 tablespoons soy sauce

1 teaspoon red chili powder

1 teaspoon sugar

½ tablespoon white vinegar

Water, as needed

8–10 small chicken drumsticks or chicken wings, skinned

1½ cups vegetable oil

1. In a large bowl, combine the ginger garlic paste, all-purpose flour, corn flour, soy sauce, red chili powder, sugar, and vinegar. Add enough water to make a thin, smooth consistency. Add the chicken and refrigerate for 3 to 4 hours.

2. In a deep pan, heat 5 to 6 tablespoons of vegetable oil. Add a few pieces of chicken to the oil, and pay-fry until crisp. If the oil begins to splatter, you can cover the pan with a splatter guard or a cover. Continue until all the pieces are cooked. Discard any remaining marinade.

3. Remove the chicken pieces and place on a paper towel to drain off any excess oil. Serve immediately.

Chicken Dressing

If you decide to use chicken wings instead of drumsticks, use just the little drumsticks of the wings. This dish is best served with the pieces all piled up on top of one another so that some of the heat is retained. Garnish with celery and carrot sticks, if desired, along with some spicy ranch dressing.

Spiced Crunchy Okra

Cocktail
Complement:

Alice in Wonderland
Green Mint Tea
(page 77)

Serves 4

1½ pounds okra, rinsed and dried
1 teaspoon red chili powder
½ teaspoon warm spice mix (see sidebar, this page)
1 teaspoon dry mango powder
3½ tablespoons chickpea flour
2 cups vegetable oil
1 teaspoon chaat spice mix
Table salt to taste

1. Remove the stems from the okra. Cut each piece lengthwise into 4 pieces. Lay out the pieces in a large, flat dish; set aside.
2. Mix the red chili powder, warm spice mix, and dry mango powder. Sprinkle this mixture over the okra. Toss well.
3. Sprinkle the chickpea flour over the okra. Toss again to ensure that each piece is lightly and evenly covered.
4. In a deep pan, add the vegetable oil to about 1 inch deep. Heat the oil over high heat until smoking. Reduce the heat to medium-high. Add some of the okra and fry until well browned. Remove and place on a paper towel to drain. Continue until all of the okra is fried. Let the oil return to its smoking point between batches.
5. Sprinkle the chaat spice mix on the okra. Toss well and season with salt. Serve immediately.

Warm Spice Mix

Mix together 2 cloves, 1 teaspoon cumin seeds, 1 green cardamom pod, 1 black cardamom pod, ½ cinnamon stick, ½ teaspoon coriander seeds, ½ teaspoon black peppercorns, and ½ bay leaf. Heat all on medium, stirring constantly for 5 minutes. Remove and allow to cool. Grind to a fine powder.

Mumbai Indian Vegetables with Rolls

Cocktail Complement:

Gretel's Hot Gingerbread Toddy (page 72)

Serves 4

1 cup cauliflower florets
¼ cup diced carrots
¼ cup diced green bell pepper
¼ cup French-cut green beans
6 tablespoons butter
1 small red onion, peeled and chopped
2 small tomatoes, chopped
1 tablespoon ginger garlic paste
2 serrano chili peppers, chopped
1 teaspoon red chili powder
¼ teaspoon turmeric powder
½ teaspoon table salt
4 medium boiled potatoes, peeled
8 square bread buns, cut horizontally
Minced cilantro, for garnish

1. In a small amount of salted water, cook the cauliflower, carrots, bell peppers, and French-cut beans together until soft. Drain, discard the water, and set the vegetables aside.

2. In a large skillet, melt 4 tablespoons of the butter over medium heat. Add the onions and sauté until transparent. Add the tomatoes and cook until the tomatoes soften, about 3 to 5 minutes. Add the ginger garlic paste and the serranos. Use a potato masher or the back of a spatula to mash the mixture. Continue cooking until you see the oil separating from the sides of the tomatoes.

3. Add the red chili powder, turmeric powder, and salt; sauté for 1 minute. Add all of the cooked vegetables and the potatoes. Continue to cook, stirring, for another 3 to 4 minutes. If the mixture starts to dry out, add 1 tablespoon of water. Remove from heat and transfer to a serving bowl.

4. Return the unrinsed skillet to the stove. Turn the heat to low. Butter the halved rolls with the remaining butter. Place the rolls buttered side down on the skillet. Toast until slightly crispy and golden brown. Remove from heat.

5. Serve the rolls alongside vegetables; garnish with cilantro.

Rolls and Bowls

Serve the vegetables in a couple of bowls so that they will stay warm for at least the first 30 minutes of your party. Create interest by making different levels with boxes with linen over the boxes. Pile the rolls all around with a side of softened butter. Make sure that you set out little plates, forks, and napkins.

South of the Border
Shrimp Cocktail

Serves 6

1 cup ketchup
2/3 cup orange juice
2 tablespoons lime juice, freshly squeezed
2 tablespoons dry white wine
2 teaspoons Worcestershire sauce
1 teaspoon hot pepper sauce
Salt and freshly ground black pepper to taste
3 cups shrimp, cooked, peeled, and deveined
6 lime wedges for garnish

Cocktail Complement:

Between the Hotel
Sheets Margarita
(page 25)

1. Whisk together the ketchup, orange juice, lime juice, wine, Worcestershire sauce, and hot pepper sauce in a large bowl. Season with salt and pepper. Taste and add more lime juice or salt if desired. Stir in the shrimp.
2. Cover and marinate in the refrigerator for at least 5 minutes or up to 4 hours before serving. To serve, divide the shrimp mixture among 6 margarita glasses. Garnish each with a lime wedge.

Smoked Horseradish Shrimp

Cocktail Complement:

Cool as a Cucumber
(page 137)

Serves 6

1 seedless cucumber, unpeeled

½ cup sour cream

¼ teaspoon prepared horseradish, drained and squeezed

1 tablespoon Dijon mustard

1 tablespoon lemon juice, freshly squeezed

1 teaspoon fresh chopped dill

¼ teaspoon freshly ground white pepper

Salt to taste

12–16 ounces smoked shrimp, chopped

Snipped fresh chives for garnish

Lemon wedges for garnish

1. Cut the cucumber into ½-inch slices. Use a small measuring spoon or melon baller to make a hollow in the center of each cucumber slice.
2. Mix together the sour cream, horseradish, Dijon, lemon juice, dill, white pepper, and salt in a bowl. Place the chopped smoked shrimp in a medium-size bowl. Add half of the horseradish dressing and toss to lightly coat. Add more dressing only if needed; be careful not to overdress.
3. Fill the hollow of each cucumber slice with the dressed shrimp, then use a melon baller to spoon a small portion of the dressed shrimp on top of the cucumber slice so that it forms a small half ball on top . Top with the snipped chives. Refrigerate until ready to serve.

Cool as a Cucumber

Try an unusual presentation by cleaning up a barbeque grill and lining the grill part with foil. Lay ruffled red or green lettuce on the foil, then place the Smoked Horseradish Shrimp on the lettuce and garnish with fresh lemon wheels. Prop the cover of the grill up and let your guests serve themselves.

Pigs in Balls

Cocktail Complement:
Mai Tai Me Up
(page 86)

Makes 50 pieces

1 pound pork sausage
½ pound Cheddar cheese, grated
4 ounces margarine, softened
5 ounces all-purpose flour
2 tablespoons paprika
Salt and freshly ground black pepper, to taste

1. Preheat oven to 350°F.
2. Form the sausage meat into fifty 1-inch balls. Place on a nonstick baking sheet and bake for 15 minutes. Transfer to paper towels to cool and drain.
3. Combine the remaining ingredients using the flat blade of an electric mixer. Wrap approximately 2 tablespoons of the dough around each sausage ball. Place the balls on an ungreased nonstick baking sheet and bake for 10 to 12 minutes, until golden. Spear with toothpicks, and serve hot.

Oink! Oink!

This hors d'oeuvre is perfect to butler around the room on a tray while they are hot or at least warm. Just make sure you supply round toothpicks for your guests to serve themselves. If you choose not to butler them, make sure that you keep in a chafing dish to keep them warm.

Spicy Potstickers

Yields 30–35 potstickers

Cocktail Complement: Who's Your Daddy? (page 87)

¼ pound fresh shrimp

½ cup canned bamboo shoots

3 medium dried mushrooms

1 cup ground pork

1½ green onions, thinly sliced

2 teaspoons Worcestershire sauce

2 teaspoons soy sauce

1 teaspoon sugar

1 teaspoon sesame oil

1 package shiu mai or potsticker wrappers (the round ones)

½ cup water for boiling potstickers

Oil for frying, as needed

1. Wash and devein the shrimp, and chop finely. Shred the bamboo shoots. Soak the dried mushrooms in hot water for at least 20 minutes to soften. Drain, remove the stems, and slice finely.

2. Combine the ground pork with the shrimp, bamboo shoots, dried mushrooms, green onions, Worcestershire sauce, soy sauce, sugar, and sesame oil.

3. To make the potstickers: Place 1 teaspoon of filling in the middle of the wrapper. Wet the edges, fold the wrapper over the filling and seal, crimping the edges. Continue with the remainder of the potstickers. Cover the completed potstickers with a damp towel to prevent drying.

4. Add 2 tablespoons oil to a preheated wok or skillet (1 tablespoon if using a nonstick pan). When oil is hot, add a few of the potstickers, smooth side down. Do not stir-fry, but let cook for about 1 minute. Do not turn the dumplings over. Add ½ cup of water and cover immediately.

5. Cook, covered, until most of the liquid is absorbed. Uncover, and cook until the liquid has evaporated. Loosen the potstickers with a spatula and serve with the browned side facing up.

Spring Rolls

Yields 12 spring rolls

½ pound pork tenderloin, shredded

2 tablespoons oyster sauce, divided

6 dried mushrooms

1 carrot

1 tablespoon chicken broth or stock

½ teaspoon sugar

1 cup mung bean sprouts, rinsed and drained

2 green onions, thinly sliced on the diagonal

¼ teaspoon sesame oil

12 spring roll wrappers

2 tablespoons plus ½ teaspoon cornstarch, divided

4–6 cups oil, for frying

Cocktail Complement:

Kama Sutra (page 97)

1. Marinate the pork in 1 tablespoon oyster sauce and ½ teaspoon cornstarch for 30 minutes.
2. Soak the dried mushrooms in hot water to soften; drain and thinly slice. Wash and grate the carrot until you have ¼ cup.
3. Combine the remaining 1 tablespoon oyster sauce, chicken broth, and sugar. Set aside. Combine remaining 2 tablespoons cornstarch with 1 tablespoon water and set aside.
4. Add 2 tablespoons oil to a preheated wok or skillet. When oil is hot, add the pork. Stir-fry briefly until it changes color and is nearly cooked through. Remove from the wok.
5. Add 1½ tablespoons oil. When oil is hot, add the dried mushrooms. Stir-fry for 1 minute, then add the bean sprouts, grated carrot, and the green onion. Add the sauce in the middle of the wok and bring to a boil. Add the pork and mix through. Drizzle with the sesame oil. Cool.
6. Heat 4 to 6 cups oil to 375°F. While oil is heating, prepare the spring rolls. To wrap, lay the wrapper in a diamond shape. Place a tablespoon of filling in the middle. Coat all the edges with the

cornstarch-and-water mixture. Roll up the wrapper and tuck in the edges. Seal the tucked-in edges with cornstarch and water. Continue with the remainder of the spring rolls. (Prepare more cornstarch and water as necessary.)

7. Deep-fry the spring rolls, 2 at a time, until they turn golden. Drain on paper towels.

Spring Forward

Spring Rolls are popular hors d'oeuvres among the masses and another great addition to an Asian-themed party. Remember that this treat takes about several bites to eat, so it's not something that you just pop into your mouth. Make sure that you provide your guests with little plates or napkins as well.

Cheesy Broiled Oysters on the Half Shell

Cocktail Complement:

Peaches and Creamtini
(page 14)

Makes 36 appetizers

36 oysters in the shell
1 teaspoon virgin olive oil
Fresh-cracked black pepper to taste
1 teaspoon lemon zest, freshly grated
¼ bunch fresh parsley, minced
Grated mozzarella cheese
Kosher salt to taste

1. Preheat oven broiler.
2. Clean and open oyster shells. Place on broiler pan and drizzle each oyster with the oil, then sprinkle with pepper and lemon zest.
3. Place under the broiler for 2 minutes. Remove and top with the cheese then cook for I minute. Top with parsley and salt, and serve.

The World Is Your Oyster

If you have a globe around, then tickle your guests' funny bones by presenting the oyster shells on a bed of curly lettuce around the globe. Another option is to present the oysters on a silver platter with white doilies. No sauce, crackers, or extra lemons are needed. Just make sure that you serve this delicacy immediately and with cocktail forks.

Stuffed Grape Leaves

Cocktail Complement:

Wine-Tasting Mama
(page 99)

Serves 6

1 small jar grape leaves
1 leek
¼ bunch fresh oregano
2 ounces feta cheese
1 teaspoon extra-virgin olive oil
1 cup white rice
1 cup basic vegetable stock
Fresh-cracked black pepper

1. Drain, rinse, and separate the grape leaves. Finely mince the leek and the oregano. Crumble the cheese.
2. Heat the oil to medium temperature in a medium-size saucepan, then add the leeks and toss them in the oil; add the rice and quickly toss again. Pour in the stock and stir. Cover and cook for approximately 15 to 20 minutes, until the rice is thoroughly cooked.
3. Cool the rice in a medium-size mixing bowl, then add the feta and pepper.
4. Lay out a grape leaf. Place a spoonful of the rice mixture on the center of the grape leaf, then fold each end over the other and seal tightly. Repeat until all the grape leaves and rice mixture are used.

Make Like a Leaf

Stuffed grape leaves will sound very interesting to your guests. Do make a little title sign, weave it through with a toothpick or bamboo skewer and stick in into one of the stuffed grape leaves. They are also a little unattractive on their own, so present on a bed of dark curly green lettuce and grapes.

Greek Fondue with White Wine

Cocktail Complement:

White Sangria
(page 112)

Serves 4–6

3/4 pound Emmenthal cheese
½ pound feta cheese
1 garlic clove
1¼ cups plus 2 tablespoons dry white wine
1 tablespoon lemon juice
1½ tablespoons cornstarch
Toasted pita bread

1. Finely dice the cheeses. Smash the garlic clove, peel, and cut in half.
2. Rub the garlic around the inside of a medium saucepan. Discard. Add 1¼ cups wine to the pan and cook on medium-low heat. Don't allow the wine to boil.
3. When the wine is warm, stir in the lemon juice. Add the cheese, a handful at a time. Stir the cheese continually in a sideways figure-eight pattern. Wait until the cheese is completely melted before adding more. Don't allow the fondue mixture to boil.
4. Dissolve the cornstarch in the remaining 2 tablespoons of wine. When the cheese is melted, stir in the cornstarch-and-wine mixture. Turn up the heat until the cheese is just bubbling and starting to thicken. Transfer to a fondue pot and set on the burner. Serve with quartered toasted pita bread for dipping.

Greek to Me

For a Greek theme, purchase a short, wide Greek column at your local craft store and some fake vines in the floral department. Place this structure in the center of your fondue table. Set the fondue pot on top of the column. Fan out cut pita wedges around the bottom column and arrange the fake vines around and up the column.

Exotic Spiked Fondue

Cocktail Complement:

Tropical Heat Wave
(page 40)

Serves 4

2 mangoes
½ pound Emmental cheese
½ pound Gruyère cheese
1 garlic clove
1¾ cups dry white wine
2 teaspoons lemon juice
½ tablespoon cornstarch
2 tablespoons kirsch

¼ teaspoon nutmeg
Black pepper to taste
1 cup mint and
    cilantro chutney
    (see sidebar, this page)
Toasted bread cubes

1. Cut the two mangoes in half, remove the pits, and cut into slices. Finely dice the cheeses.
2. Smash the garlic, peel, and cut in half. Rub the garlic around the inside of a medium saucepan. Discard. Add the wine to the pan and cook on low heat. Don't allow the wine to boil.
3. When the wine is warm, stir in the lemon juice. Add the cheese, a handful at a time. Stir the cheese continually. Wait until the cheese is completely melted before adding more. Don't allow the fondue mixture to boil.
4. When the cheese is melted, dissolve the cornstarch in the kirsch and stir into the cheese. Turn up the heat until it just bubbles and starts to thicken. Stir in the nutmeg and black pepper. Add the chutney.
5. Transfer to a fondue pot and set on the burner. Serve with the bread cubes and sliced mangoes for dipping.

Mint Condition

To make mint and cilantro chutney, mix 3 bunches chopped cilantro, 1 small bunch fresh chopped mint, 2 minced garlic cloves, 1½ tablespoons freshly grated ginger, 1 to 2 finely chopped serrano chilies, ½ teaspoon salt, juice of 1 small lemon, and ½ tablespoon peanut oil.

Drunken Ham-and-Cheese Fondue

Serves 4–5

1¼ pounds medium Cheddar cheese
1 baguette
1½ cups cooked ham
1 green onion
1 tablespoon butter or margarine
1 cup beer
1 teaspoon lemon juice
1 tablespoon cornstarch
1½ tablespoons water
1 teaspoon kirsch
2 teaspoons Worcestershire sauce
1/8 teaspoon black pepper, or to taste

Cocktail
Complement:
Screwdriver
(page 127)

1. Cut the cheddar cheese into cubes and set aside. Slice the baguette into cubes and set aside. Cut the cooked ham into cubes. Dice the green onion.
2. Heat the butter in a medium saucepan. Add the beer and warm on low heat. When the beer is warm, add the lemon juice. Add the cheese gradually, stirring continually in a sideways figure-eight pattern until it is completely melted.
3. When the cheese is melted, dissolve the cornstarch in the water and add to the cheese, stirring. Turn up the heat until it is just bubbling and starting to thicken. Add the kirsch, the Worcestershire sauce, and the black pepper. Taste and adjust the seasonings if desired.
4. Transfer the cheese to a fondue pot and set on the burner. Invite guests to place a baguette cube and a piece of ham on their fork before dipping into the fondue.

Hawaiian Luau
Chocolate Chip Fondue

Cocktail Complement:
Swirl from Ipanema
(page 37)

Serves 6

1 pineapple, cut into triangle slices
2 cups chocolate chips
½ cup half-and-half or light cream
3 tablespoons honey
1 teaspoon cinnamon
½ teaspoon nutmeg
¼ teaspoon ground cloves, or to taste
15–20 small cookies (of your choice)
Bamboo skewers

1. Refrigerate the pineapple slices.
2. Combine the chocolate chips and cream in a metal bowl and place on top of a saucepan half-filled with simmering water. Add the honey. Melt the chocolate on low to medium-low heat, making sure it doesn't boil.
3. When the chocolate is melted, stir in the cinnamon, nutmeg, and ground cloves. Skewer the pineapple triangles so a tip of the pineapple is pointing up. Garnish fondue pot with the pineapple skewers and cookies for dipping.

Tropical Melon

This fondue would be excellent at a Hawaiian luau! For a festive presentation, cut a watermelon in half, set flat side down on cloth napkins, and stick the pineapple skewers (with pineapple side up) into the watermelon. Place a fondue pot in the middle of the two watermelon halves, then arrange the cookies all around. Decorate with some leis or tropical flowers.

Cheeseburger-in-Paradise Pizza Fondue

Cocktail Complement:

Beer Belly Margarita
(page 26)

Serves 4–6

1/3 pound ground beef

2 tablespoons olive oil

1 medium yellow onion, peeled and chopped

3/4 cup milk

1½ pounds Monterey jack cheese, shredded

1 cup tomato sauce

¼ teaspoon dried basil

¼ teaspoon dried oregano

1 pineapple, sliced and diced

6 pepperoni slices

20 black olives, or as desired

Pickles, as needed

Soft Italian breadsticks, for dipping

1. Brown the ground beef in a frying pan. Drain and set aside.
2. In a medium saucepan, heat the olive oil. Add the onion and sauté until it is tender. Add the milk and warm on medium-low heat.
3. Add the cheese, a handful at a time. Stir the cheese continually in a sideways figure-eight pattern. Wait until the cheese is completely melted before adding more. Don't allow the fondue mixture to boil.
4. When the cheese is nearly melted, add the tomato sauce, ground beef, and pepperoni and heat through. Turn up the heat until the fondue is just bubbling and starting to thicken. Add the basil and oregano. Transfer to a fondue pot, and set on the burner. Serve with the olives, pickles, pineapple, and breadsticks for dipping.

Filet Mignon Calzones

Cocktail Complement:

Blue Velvetini
(page 15)

Serves 4

1½ pounds pizza dough
2 tablespoons olive oil
½ cup onion, minced
1 tablespoon flour
½ cup beef broth
3/4 pound filet mignon, sliced thinly
4 slices white American cheese

1. Roll the dough into 4 rounds, each 6 to 7 inches across.
2. Heat the olive oil in a saucepan, then add the minced onion and sauté. Blend in the flour, then stir in the beef broth and cook until smooth.
3. Add the filet and cook for 1 minute. Spoon the filling onto the bottom half of each round of dough, adding one slice of cheese to each. Fold the top over and seal with a fork.
4. Bake the calzones on a pizza stone in a covered grill for about 6 minutes, or until very hot and golden brown.

Just Say Filet!

Calzones embedded with filet mignon should be presented with nothing less than a gold or silver platter. To bump it up a step, arrange on a bed of crisp white doilies. If you don't have the doilies, substitute a bed of curly red or green lettuce and sprigs of grapes for a garnish.

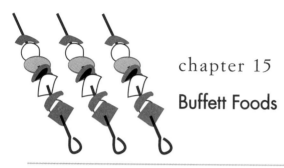

chapter 15

Buffett Foods

Shiitake Chardonnay Fettuccine

Cocktail Complement:
Lemon Raspberry Rita (page 27)

Serves 4

4 ounces (1 stick) unsalted butter, divided
½ teaspoon kosher salt
3 leaves fresh sage or a pinch of dried
1 pound shiitake mushrooms, stems removed, sliced thin
¼ cup dry white wine
¼ cup vegetable stock or water
8 ounces (½ box) fettuccine, cooked
¼ cup roughly chopped Italian parsley
Juice of 1 lemon, plus 6 lemon wedges

1. Place all but 1 tablespoon of the butter in a large skillet with the salt. Cook over medium heat until the butter turns brown and has a smoky, nutty aroma—it should not turn black or smell burnt.
2. Add the sage, and then the mushrooms. Cook without stirring for 5 minutes, to brown the mushrooms. Stir; cook until the mushrooms are wilted and juicy.
3. Add the wine. Cook 1 minute to steam out the alcohol. Add the stock, cooked fettuccine, parsley, and lemon juice. Remove from heat, add remaining 1 tablespoon butter, and toss to coat. Serve with extra lemon wedges.

Whiny Fettuccine

The Stuffed Mediterranean Mushrooms (page 165) would make a great appetizer and nice complement to this Shiitake Chardonnay Fettuccine. To avoid overcooking the fettuccine, serve this dish directly on plates from the skillet, or transfer directly to a nice serving bowl. Sliced bread with butter makes a nice addition.

Black Olive Angel Hair Broccoli

Serves 6

1 pound fresh fava beans, shelled (about 1 cup),
   or 1 cup fresh or frozen green peas

1 tablespoon olive oil

2 cloves garlic, finely chopped

Pinch of crush red pepper flakes (optional)

¼ cup black olives, pitted

1 bunch broccoli rabe, cut into bite-sized pieces, blanched

1 box (1 pound) angel hair pasta

1 tablespoon butter

¼ cup grated Parmesan cheese

¼ pound block pecorino, feta, or other semihard cheese

Lemon wedges

Cocktail Complement:

White Sangria
(page 112)

1. Bring a large pot of salted water to a rolling boil. Drop the fava beans in for 2 minutes. Skim them out with a slotted spoon, and shock them by plunging them into ice-cold water. Peel off the outer leathery skin. Set them aside. Keep the water at a rolling boil.

2. Heat the oil in a large skillet over medium heat. Add the garlic, pepper flakes, and olives, and cook, stirring, until the garlic begins to brown. Add the broccoli rabe; cook until heated through, about 2 minutes. Turn off heat.

3. Put the angel hair pasta into the boiling water, stir well to separate, and cook until tender, about 2 minutes—it cooks very quickly. Drain and add to the skillet, allowing some of the water from the pasta to drip into the pan. Toss with butter and Parmesan; season to taste. Using a swivel vegetable peeler, shave pecorino cheese liberally over pasta. Serve with lemon wedges.

Pumpkin Spinach Lasagna

Cocktail
Complement:
You Don't Know
Jack o'Lantern Punch
(page 104)

Serves 8

1 pound lasagna

1 tablespoon salt

1 small pumpkin (2–3 pounds)

¼ teaspoon crushed red pepper flakes

¼ teaspoon ground nutmeg

2 tablespoons olive oil

3 cloves garlic, chopped

1 large bunch spinach (or 6-ounce cello bag), washed thoroughly

2 pounds ricotta

1 egg

4 ounces Parmesan cheese, grated

4 ounces mozzarella or provolone cheese, grated

2 cups tomato sauce

1. Cook lasagna to not quite al dente, according to directions on box. Rinse and drain. Toss with a drop of olive oil. Set aside. Refill pasta pot with 3 quarts water, add 1 tablespoon salt, and bring to a boil.
2. Peel pumpkin: Cut off the top and bottom and shave the outside with a knife, always shaving downward, toward the cutting board; a potato peeler can also be used. Discard seeds and cube pumpkin into bite-size pieces. Boil pumpkin pieces 15 minutes, until tender, in salted water. Drain, and toss with crushed pepper and nutmeg.
3. In a 10-inch skillet, sauté half of the garlic in 1 tablespoon olive oil, adding half of the spinach when garlic starts to brown. Allow spinach to wilt, then turn out onto a plate, and repeat with remaining spinach and garlic. Season with salt and pepper. Mix the ricotta, egg, and Parmesan together. Set aside.

4. Assemble the lasagna in layers, starting with noodle, then cheese mixture, then spinach and pumpkin. Make 2 more layers, making sure to save unbroken lasagna for the top layer. Sprinkle grated mozzarella or provolone on top.

5. Bake 30 minutes at 400°F until brown and bubbling on top. Let rest 15 minutes before serving with tomato sauce on the side.

Carriage Lasagna

Start guests off with the Fairy-Tale Fondue (page 146). Simply add more pumpkin-dipping bread to the appetizer so that it ties together the pumpkin theme. Decorate all around with pumpkins and other autumn items. You can serve the Pumpkin Spinach Lasagna from a chafing dish, allowing guests to serve themselves.

Wild Almond Apple Rice

Cocktail Complement:

Almond Joytini
(page 20)

Serves 8

½ cup wild rice

½ cup shelled almonds, whole or in slivers

1 tablespoon oil

1 large onion, roughly chopped

1 Rome or Golden Delicious apple, peeled, cored, and diced

¼ cup raisins

Salt and freshly ground black pepper to taste

1 tablespoon olive oil (or butter)

¼ cup chopped cilantro or parsley

1. Boil the rice in 2½ quarts salted water until tender, about 40 minutes; drain, saving cooking liquid. Toast the almonds until fragrant and visibly shiny. Heat the oil in a large skillet or Dutch oven over medium heat for 1 minute. Add onions; cook until softened, about 5 minutes. Add the apples, raisins, and a splash of the rice-cooking liquid. Cook 5 minutes more, until the apples are translucent.
2. Combine the cooked rice, the apple mixture, the nuts, and salt and pepper. Stir in olive oil (or butter), if desired, and serve garnished with cilantro or parsley.

Nice Rice

Although this dish is excellent served by itself, it can be a nice complement to the Sweet-and-Sour Pork (page 238), Candied Ginger Cashew Chicken (page 239), or Hawaiian Stuffed Macadamia Pork (page 259). You can start your guests off with a nice hors d'oeuvre such as the Stuffed Sweet Peppers (page 200) or the Strawberry Brie Chutney (page 199).

Berry Good Noodles

Cocktail Complement:

Berry Bordello
(page 85)

Serves 4

Juice of 1 lemon

3 tablespoons fruit-flavored brandy

2 cups mixed berries, such as blueberries, strawberries, and raspberries

½ pound medium egg noodles

1/3 cup powdered sugar

3/4 cup half-and-half

¼ cup walnuts, coarsely chopped and toasted

1. In a cup, combine the lemon juice and brandy. Place the berries in a shallow bowl and sprinkle with the sugar and lemon juice/brandy mixture. Cover and chill for 2 hours.
2. In a large pot, bring at least 4 quarts water to a rolling boil. Add 1 tablespoon salt. Add the pasta, stir to separate, and cook until al dente. Drain.
3. Place the half-and-half in a saucepan large enough to hold the noodles. Add the noodles and toss over low heat. Transfer to a warm serving dish. Top with the berries and sprinkle with the nuts.

Oodles of Noodles

The Berry Good Noodles are very colorful. Transfer the dish to a clear bowl or a silver platter. If you decide to use a bowl, then whole strawberries can be pressed on the lip of the bowl all the way around the rim. If you'd like to serve an hors d'oeuvre before this dish, then serve the Strawberry Brie Chutney (page 199).

Champagne Angel Scallops

Cocktail Complement:

Pear Phero Moan
(page 85)

Serves 4

1 bottle inexpensive dry (brut) champagne
1/3 cup white wine vinegar
1/3 cup minced shallots
4 cups (1 quart) heavy cream
2 tablespoons fresh lemon juice
1 teaspoon salt
1 teaspoon pepper, freshly ground
3/4 pound bay scallops
1 pound angel hair pasta
2 tablespoons chopped parsley

1. Combine the champagne, vinegar, and shallots in a 6-quart sauce-pan over high heat. Reduce to 2 cups. Add the cream, and reduce to 3½ cups, or until thickened to the consistency of light gravy. Be careful not to reduce too much, or the butter will separate from the cream. Add the lemon juice, salt, pepper, and scallops to the sauce and heat until the scallops are cooked, 2 to 3 minutes.
2. Meanwhile, in a large pot, bring at least 4 quarts of water to a rolling boil. Add 1 tablespoon salt. Add the pasta, stir to separate, and cook until al dente. Drain.
3. Add the pasta to the sauce, and toss to coat well and heat through. Sprinkle with parsley.

Cherub Scallops

Serve the Champagne Angel Scallops on a warm serving platter and sprinkle with the parsley. This dish is best served with guests sitting down at the table or with the pasta in a chafing dish at an angels-and-devils–themed party.

Lemon Vodka Fettuccine

Cocktail Complement:

Lemondrop
(page 123)

Serves 4

1 pound fettuccine
1 tablespoon salt
1 tablespoon unsalted butter, if needed

Lemon Vodka Sauce

1 cup heavy cream
½ cup vodka
Juice of 1 lemon
Zest of 1 lemon, finely grated
2 tablespoons chopped fresh chives
½ teaspoon pepper, freshly ground
2 tablespoons chopped parsley
3/4 cup Parmesan cheese, freshly grated

1. In a large pot, bring at least 4 quarts water to a rolling boil. Add the salt. Add the pasta, stir to separate, and cook until al dente. Drain. If the sauce is not ready at this point, toss the pasta with the butter and set aside in a warm bowl.
2. Make the sauce: In a large, deep skillet, combine the cream and vodka and simmer until the sauce thickens a little, about 5 minutes. Add the lemon juice, zest, chives, and pepper and cook for 1 minute, stirring constantly. Do not allow the sauce to boil.
3. Add the pasta to the skillet and combine with the sauce so that all the strands are well coated. Garnish with the parsley. Pass the Parmesan cheese at the table.

Peanut Vermicelli Stir-Fry

Cocktail Complement:

Hunka Hunka
Burnin' Love
(page 60)

Serves 4

Pasta

1 pound vermicelli pasta
Vegetable oil for pasta,
    if needed, plus 1 teaspoon
2 cups broccoli florets
1 large red bell pepper,
    seeded and finely julienned
1 bunch scallions,
    cut on the diagonal
    into ½-inch lengths
½ teaspoon dried hot red
    pepper flakes, or to taste

Sauce

3 tablespoons creamy
    peanut butter
1/3 cup fresh lime juice
¼ cup soy sauce
¼ cup chicken stock

1. Make the sauce: In a small bowl, whisk together the peanut butter, lime juice, soy sauce, and stock. Season with pepper.
2. In a large pot, bring at least 4 quarts water to a rolling boil. Add 1 tablespoon salt. Add the pasta, stir to separate, and cook until al dente. Drain. Transfer to a warm bowl and toss with a bit of the oil if the sauce is not ready.
3. Meanwhile, place a large, deep skillet or a wok over high heat and heat the oil. Add the broccoli and bell pepper and stir-fry briefly. The vegetables should remain crisp. Add the scallions and red pepper flakes, then stir-fry for 2 minutes.

Nutty Pasta

The Peanut Vermicelli Stir-Fry will need to be served immediately so that the pasta doesn't begin sticking together. Serve the pasta in a bowl and the stir fry in another with a large spoon. Great starters for this dish include Fried Green Tomato Bruschetta (page 186), Italian Steering Wheels (page 191), or Spiced Crunchy Okra (page 205).

Black Bean Cherry Tomato Bow Ties

Cocktail Complement:

Black Martini
(page 17)

Serves 4

2 teaspoons olive oil or vegetable oil
2 cloves garlic, finely chopped
1 bunch scallions, trimmed and thinly sliced, including green tops
1½ teaspoons ground cumin
1½ tablespoons fresh lemon juice
1 15-ounce can black beans, well rinsed and drained
Salt and freshly ground pepper to taste
3/4 pound bow tie pasta
8 cherry tomatoes, quartered
2 tablespoons chopped fresh cilantro

1. In a saucepan, heat the oil over medium heat. Add the garlic and sauté until soft, just a few minutes. Do not allow to brown. Add the scallions and cumin and cook briefly.
2. Remove from the heat and stir in the lemon juice. Add the beans and toss to coat. Season with salt and pepper.
3. In a large pot, bring 4 quarts water to a rolling boil. Add 1 tablespoon salt. Add the pasta, and cook until just under al dente. Reserve ½ cup of the cooking water. Drain and return the pasta to the pot.
4. Add the reserved pasta water to the black bean mixture, stir, and add to the pasta. Bring to a boil over medium heat and cook until the sauce is thick enough to coat the pasta. Remove from the heat. Carefully stir in the cherry tomatoes and cilantro just before serving.

Black-Tie Event

Serve this dish in a clear bowl so that all the beautiful colors and shapes can be seen. Decorate the top of the bowl by placing cherry tomatoes lined up around the rim. You can also add whole pitted black olives and alternate the colors.

Shrimp Artichoke Spirals

Cocktail Complement:

White Sangriarita
(page 25)

Serves 4

2 packages frozen artichoke hearts
48 large shrimp, peeled and deveined
2 egg yolks
1 cup extra-virgin olive oil
½ cup peanut oil
½ cup wine vinegar
4 tablespoons Dijon mustard
¼ cup chopped fresh parsley
¼ cup scallions, sliced, including green parts
2 tablespoons minced shallots
Salt and freshly ground black pepper to taste
¾ pound spirals (fusilli) pasta

1. Cook the artichokes according to package directions.
2. Bring 4 quarts of water to boil. Add 1 tablespoon salt. Add shrimp all at once. When the water returns to a boil, cook until shrimp turn pink, less than 5 minutes, depending on size of shrimp. Drain.
3. Place olive and peanut oils, vinegar, and mustard in a mixing bowl. Beat with a whisk to blend. Stir in parsley, scallions, and shallots. Add salt and pepper to taste.
4. Place shrimp and artichokes in a large bowl. Pour sauce over to cover. Reserve remaining sauce. Refrigerate to marinate for at least 2 hours or overnight.
5. When ready to serve, bring at least 4 quarts of water to a rolling boil. Add a tablespoon of salt. Cook pasta until al dente.
6. Transfer pasta to a large bowl. Pour shrimp and artichoke mixture over pasta, add reserved sauce, and toss. Serve cold or at room temperature. The shrimp and artichoke mixture can be added to the pasta ahead of time, but the reserved sauce should be added just before serving.

Smoked Angel Hair Salmon

Cocktail Complement:

Sparkling New Year Cheer (page 96)

Serves 4

2 cups heavy cream

1 cup milk

2 tablespoons chopped fresh dill

½ cup chopped scallions

2 teaspoons lemon zest, freshly grated

3 tablespoons capers, drained

Salt and freshly ground pepper to taste

1 pound angel hair pasta

6 ounces smoked salmon, thinly sliced, cut into thin strips

1. Combine the cream, milk, dill, scallions, and lemon zest in heavy-bottomed saucepan. Bring to a boil over medium-high heat. Reduce to a simmer and cook briefly until thickened. Stir in the capers. Season with salt and pepper.
2. Meanwhile, in a large pot, bring at least 4 quarts of water to a rolling boil. Add 1 tablespoon salt. Add the pasta, stir to separate, and cook until al dente.
3. Drain, and transfer the pasta to a large, warm bowl. Pour the sauce over it and toss to coat. Add the smoked salmon and toss again to combine. Serve.

Smoking Angel

Start off with the Smoked Salmon Cucumbers from Chapter 13 or with the Filet Mignon Calzones, Brie and Papaya Quesadillas, or Strawberry Brie Chutney from Chapter 14. Try to serve the Smoked Angel Hair Salmon at a table setting because this dish should be served warm.

Mushroom Chicken Cacciatore

Cocktail Complement:

Sangria
(page 113)

Serves 6

¼ cup vegetable oil

1 3½ pound chicken, cut into serving pieces

1 cup onions, finely chopped

½ pound fresh mushrooms, thinly sliced

1 clove garlic, minced

1 28-ounce can Italian plum tomatoes, with juice

½ cup dry red wine

1 teaspoon dried oregano

1 bay leaf, crumbled

1 pound rotelli pasta

1 tablespoon salt

½ cup chopped parsley

1. In a large, deep skillet, heat the oil over moderately high heat. Pat the chicken dry and brown it in batches. Do not crowd the pan. Transfer to a bowl.
2. Pour off all but about 3 tablespoons of oil. Add the onions and mushrooms and sauté until the onions are golden. Add the garlic and cook 1 minute. Add the tomatoes with juice, wine, chicken and any juices that have accumulated in the bowl, oregano, and bay leaf, and simmer, covered, stirring occasionally and breaking up the tomatoes, for 30 to 35 minutes, or until the chicken is tender.
3. Meanwhile, in a large pot, bring at least 4 quarts of water to a rolling boil. Add 1 tablespoon of salt. Add the rotelli and stir to prevent sticking. Cook until al dente. Drain.
4. Transfer the pasta to the skillet and toss with the sauce to coat. Garnish with the parsley.

Cashew Corn Chowder

Cocktail
Complement:
Candy Corn
(page 48)

Serves 4

4 teaspoons canola oil

1 large sweet onion, chopped

4 stalks celery, chopped

1 medium-sized sweet potato, peeled and diced

3 cloves garlic, minced

1 tablespoon unbleached all-purpose flour

6 cups water

1 10-ounce package sweet corn, thawed

1 small red bell pepper, seeded and diced

1 small green bell pepper, seeded and diced

½ cup no-salt-added roasted cashew butter

1 tablespoon fresh lime juice

1 teaspoon dried cilantro, crushed

1/16 teaspoon cayenne

1/8 teaspoon freshly ground black pepper

1. Heat the oil in a large saucepan on medium-high. Add the onions and celery; sauté for 3 to 4 minutes, stirring frequently. Add the sweet potatoes; sauté for 1 or 2 minutes, stirring to blend with the onions and celery. Add the garlic and sauté for 1 minute.
2. Lower the heat to medium and stir in the flour. Continue to stir for 5 minutes to completely cook the flour. Add the water and bring to a boil; reduce the heat, cover the pot, and simmer for 40 minutes or until the sweet potatoes are completely tender. Stir well, mashing the sweet potatoes somewhat with the back of a spoon or use a hand blender to cream the soup.
3. Stir in the corn. Return the cover to the pan and simmer for 20 more minutes.
4. Add the bell peppers; cover and simmer for 5 minutes. Add the cashew butter, stirring to blend it completely. Stir in the lime juice, cilantro, cayenne, and pepper. Serve warm.

Sweet-and-Sour Pork

Cocktail Complement:

Blue Hawaiian
(page 120)

Serves 4

1 large white or yellow onion, cut into large dice

1 large green bell pepper, seeded and chopped

1 clove garlic, minced

1/8 cup (2 tablespoons) dry sherry or pork broth or water

½ pound cooked pork, shredded

¼ cup Mr. Spice Sweet & Sour Sauce

1. In a medium-size microwave-safe bowl, combine the onion, pepper, garlic, and sherry; microwave on high for 3 minutes or until the vegetables are crisp-tender.

2. Add the sweet-and-sour sauce and pork; stir to combine. Cover and microwave at 70 percent power for 2 minutes or until the mixture is heated through. Taste and add more sweet-and-sour sauce, if desired.

Yin and Yang Pork

Try serving this dish at a yin/yang-themed party, where everything is opposite. Sweet and sour, good and bad, black and white. . . . Who knows what your guests will come up with. Maybe serve a Black Martini (page 17) and a White Chocolatini (page 14). You could combine this party with a costume Halloween party as well.

Candied Ginger Cashew Chicken

Cocktail Complement:
Charming Proposal
(page 91)

Serves 4

1 tablespoon water or chicken broth or lemon juice
1 small sweet onion, chopped
1 clove garlic, chopped
4 cups broccoli florets
1 pound cooked dark meat chicken
6 tablespoons Mr. Spice Ginger Stir-Fry Sauce
¼ cup unsalted dry-roasted cashew pieces
Optional: candied ginger, minced

1. In a large microwave-safe bowl, combine the water, onion, garlic, and broccoli. Cover and microwave on high for 4 minutes or until the broccoli is crisp-tender. Add the chicken and stir-fry sauce; stir well.
2. Microwave at 70 percent power for 2 minutes or until the mixture is heated through. Serve over cooked rice; top each serving with 1 tablespoon of the cashews, and minced candied ginger, if desired.

Metallic Holiday

To decorate for a holiday party, you will need some gold or silver paint, newspaper, and some foliage from your yard. Simply break off some leafy bush pieces, spread them on the newspaper, and spray with the paint. Sturdy leaves work best. Coat completely or just spray little tinges of paint on the foliage. Place around the room.

Chicken Skillet Casserole

Cocktail Complement:
Sloe Screw
(page 128)

Serves 4

½ cup skim milk

2 tablespoons Hellmann's or
*   Best Foods Real Mayonnaise*

1 cup water

½ teaspoon Minor's Low Sodium Chicken Base

¼ cup Maple Leaf Potato Granules
*   (or other unseasoned, no-fat-added*
*   instant mashed potato flakes or potato flour)*

½ teaspoon onion powder

¼ teaspoon garlic powder

¼ teaspoon dried celery flakes

1/8 teaspoon freshly ground black pepper

1 large egg, beaten

1 teaspoon Lea & Perrins Worcestershire Sauce

1 tablespoon lemon juice

1 10-ounce package frozen vegetables blend, thawed

1 cup sliced button mushrooms

½ pound cooked chicken, chopped

1 1/3 cups cooked brown, long-grain rice

1. Add the milk, mayonnaise, water, chicken base, potato granules, onion powder, garlic powder, celery flakes, pepper, egg, Worcestershire sauce, and lemon juice to a blender or the bowl of a food processor; pulse until well mixed.

2. Pour the mixture into a large, deep nonstick sauté pan; bring to a boil. Reduce heat and simmer, stirring until the mixture begins to thicken.

3. Add the frozen vegetables, mushrooms, and chicken; stir to combine. Cover and simmer for 5 minutes or until the mushrooms are cooked. Serve over rice.

Black Forest Sausage Sauerkraut

Cocktail Complement:
Sugar and Spice and Everything Nice
(page 73)

Serves 6

2½ pounds fresh Polish sausage
6 medium carrots
6 medium potatoes
2 medium yellow onions
3 cloves garlic
4 cups sauerkraut
1½ cups dry white wine
1 teaspoon caraway seeds
½ teaspoon ground black pepper

1. Cut the Polish sausage into 3-inch pieces. Peel the carrots and cut into 3-inch lengths. Peel the potatoes and cut into 1-inch cubes. Peel the onions and cut into ¼-inch rings. Peel the garlic and mince with a sharp kitchen knife. Rinse and drain the sauerkraut.
2. Brown the sausage in a skillet at medium-high heat; drain off grease and transfer sausage to the slow cooker. Add remaining ingredients to the slow cooker. Cover and cook on low setting for 8 to 9 hours.

Halloween Sheets

An inexpensive costume and decorating idea for a Halloween party is to head to your local hotel. Hotels have mounds of torn and stained sheets that they throw away. Simply tell them that you are looking to make some costumes and ask them to give you their old sheets. Dye and cut them up however you want.

Garbanzo Sausage

Cocktail Complement:
Melontini
(page 12)

Serves 4

1 *medium-sized white onion*
1 *garlic clove*
2 *cups canned garbanzo beans*
½ *cup canned pimientos*
½ *pound pork sausage*
1 *teaspoon chili powder*
½ *teaspoon salt*
¼ *teaspoon dried oregano*
½ *teaspoon ground black pepper*

1. Peel the onion and chop into ¼-inch pieces. Peel and mince the garlic. Drain the garbanzo beans and rinse. Drain the pimientos and cut into ¼-inch-wide strips.
2. Brown the sausage in a frying pan on medium heat. Add the onion, garlic, and chili powder; cook until the onion is soft.
3. Add the garbanzos and pimientos; stir well. Bring to a simmer. Add the salt, oregano, and pepper.

Stoplight Peppers

Serve Garbanzo Sausage individually by hollowing out green, yellow, or red peppers and really jazz up this dish. Cut off the top of a pepper, clean out the seeds, fill with Garbanzo Sausage, then set the pepper cap back on top. For a fun twist, try setting different-colored pepper caps on different peppers.

Mexican Beer Beans

Cocktail
Complement:
Anita Rita Now
(page 29)

Serves 6

2 cups dry pinto beans
2 cups dark Mexican beer
2 slices bacon
1 medium onion
3 garlic cloves
2 large red tomatoes
4 pickled jalapeño chilies
1 teaspoon salt
1 teaspoon ground black pepper

1. Soak the pinto beans in 6 cups of water overnight. Drain and rinse. Put the beans into a large pot and cover with water. Bring to a boil, then reduce heat. Simmer for 30 minutes or until the beans are cooked but still firm. Drain off water and add the beer. Stir and continue to cook on low heat.
2. Fry the bacon until very crisp. Reserve the grease in the frying pan. Transfer the bacon to a paper towel to cool. When cool, crumble into pieces about ¼-inch square.
3. Peel the onion and chop into ¼-inch pieces. Peel and mince the garlic. Remove the stems from the tomatoes and chop into ½-inch pieces. Remove the stems from the jalapeños and chop into ¼-inch pieces.
4. Add the onion and garlic to the bacon grease. Cook until the onion is clear and limp. Add the tomato and jalapeños; stir to blend. Cook for about 5 minutes.
5. Add the tomato mixture to the beans. Stir in the crumbled bacon, salt, and pepper. Bring to a boil, reduce heat to low, and simmer for about 15 minutes.

Spicy Cashew Chicken

Cocktail Complement:
Sex with the Captain
(page 43)

Serves 2–4

2 boneless, skinless chicken breasts

2 tablespoons dark soy sauce

1 tablespoon Chinese rice wine or dry sherry

1 teaspoon sugar

¼ teaspoon sesame oil

¼ teaspoon chili paste

3 tablespoons oil for stir-frying

½ cup cashews

1. Cut the chicken into 1-inch cubes. Mix together the dark soy sauce, rice wine, sugar, sesame oil, and chili paste, and set aside.
2. Add 2 tablespoons oil to a preheated wok or skillet. Stir-fry the chicken until it is nearly cooked through. Remove, then drain on paper towels.
3. Wipe the wok clean with a paper towel and add 1 tablespoon of oil. Stir-fry the cashews very briefly, until they are golden.
4. Add the sauce to the wok and bring it to a boil. Turn down the heat and add the chicken back to the wok. Mix thoroughly and serve hot.

Color Me Happy

A color cocktail party is a very popular fun time. Basically, the host chooses a color for everyone to wear to the party. The host also matches invitations, food and drink, and decorations to the chosen color theme. You can also combine other parties with a color theme. For example, you can have a pink baby shower.

Moo Goo Guy & Doll Pan

Cocktail Complement:

Anita Rita Now (page 29)

Serves 4

2 large boneless, skinless chicken breasts
4 tablespoons oyster sauce, divided
2 teaspoons cornstarch, divided
½ cup chicken stock or broth
1 teaspoon sugar
1/8 teaspoon white pepper
½ cup fresh mushrooms
4 tablespoons oil for stir-frying
1 clove garlic, minced
4 ounces (half of an 8-ounce can) bamboo shoots, rinsed

1. Rinse the chicken, pat dry, and cut into thin slices. Mix together 2 tablespoons of the oyster sauce and 1 teaspoon cornstarch. Marinate the chicken in mixture for 30 minutes.

2. Mix together the chicken stock, sugar, white pepper, remaining 2 tablespoons oyster sauce, and 1 teaspoon cornstarch. Set aside. Wipe the mushrooms clean with a damp cloth and thinly slice.

3. Add 2 tablespoons oil to a preheated wok or skillet. When oil is hot, add the garlic and stir-fry briefly until aromatic. Add the chicken and stir-fry until it changes color and is nearly cooked through. Remove the chicken from the wok and set aside.

4. Wipe the wok clean and add 2 more tablespoons oil. When the oil is hot, add the mushrooms and stir-fry for about 1 minute. Add the bamboo shoots.

5. Give the sauce a quick stir. Make a well in the middle of the wok by pushing the vegetables up to the sides. Add the sauce in the middle, stirring vigorously to thicken. Add the chicken and mix through.

Sherry Beef Curry

Serves 2–4

½ pound beef sirloin

2 teaspoons dry sherry

1 teaspoon cornstarch

2 ounces rice-stick noodles

1 tablespoon curry paste

¼ teaspoon turmeric

¼ teaspoon ground cumin

3 tablespoons oil for stir-frying

2 teaspoons minced ginger

1 teaspoon minced garlic

2 tablespoons chopped red onion

1 tablespoon plain yogurt

Cocktail Complement:

White Russian (page 129)

1. Cut the beef across the grain into thin strips about 1½ inches in length. Add the rice wine and cornstarch (in that order). Marinate the beef for 1 hour.
2. Soak the rice noodles in hot water for 15 minutes or until they are softened. Drain thoroughly.
3. Mix together the curry paste, turmeric, and ground cumin.
4. Add 2 tablespoons oil to a preheated wok or skillet. When oil is hot, add the ginger and garlic and stir-fry briefly until aromatic. Add the beef. Stir-fry until it changes color and is nearly cooked through. Remove from the wok and drain on paper towels.
5. Add 1 tablespoon oil to the wok. When oil is hot, add the curry paste mixture and stir-fry briefly until it is aromatic. Add the onion and stir-fry until it is soft and translucent. Add the rice-stick noodles and mix with the onion. Add 2 tablespoons water if necessary. Add the meat and the yogurt. Mix everything together and cook until the meat is cooked through.

Mongolian Baby Corn Beef

Cocktail Complement: Bermuda Triangle Tea (page 41)

Serves 4

1 pound sirloin or flank steak
1 egg white
Pinch of salt
1½ teaspoons sesame oil, divided
1 tablespoon cornstarch
1½ tablespoons oil
2 green onions
2 garlic cloves, minced
½ teaspoon chili sauce
1 can baby corn, rinsed and drained

1 tablespoon Chinese rice wine
    or dry sherry
2 tablespoons hoisin sauce
1 tablespoon dark soy sauce
½ teaspoon sugar
1½ teaspoons cornstarch

1. Slice the beef across the grain into thin strips. Add the egg white, salt, 1 teaspoon sesame oil, and cornstarch to the beef, adding the cornstarch last. Marinate the beef for 30 minutes. Add 1½ tablespoons oil and marinate for another 30 minutes.

2. While beef is marinating, cut the green onions into thirds on the diagonal.

3. Add 1 cup oil to a preheated wok or skillet. When oil is hot, carefully slide the beef into the wok, a few pieces at a time. Fry the beef until it changes color. Remove from the wok with a slotted spoon and drain on paper towels.

4. Remove all but 2 tablespoons of oil. When oil is hot, add the garlic and chili sauce. Stir-fry briefly until the garlic is aromatic. Add the baby corn.

5. Add the beef back to the wok. Add the rice wine, hoisin sauce, dark soy sauce, and sugar. Mix the cornstarch and water, and add to the middle of the wok, stirring vigorously to thicken. Mix all the ingredients together thoroughly. Stir in the green onion. Drizzle with ½ teaspoon sesame oil and serve hot.

Spicy Sour Rice Noodles

Cocktail Complement:
Tootsie Rolltini
(page 21)

Serves 4–6

¼ pound rice-stick noodles

¼ cup dark soy sauce

1 teaspoon sugar

¼ teaspoon hot chili oil

1/8 teaspoon salt

1/8 teaspoon freshly ground Szechwan peppercorns

¼ teaspoon chili paste

1 teaspoon black rice vinegar

½ cup water

1½ tablespoons oil for stir-frying

¼ cup chopped onion

1. Soak the rice-stick noodles in hot water for 15 minutes, or until they are softened. Drain thoroughly.
2. Combine the dark soy sauce, sugar, Hot Chili Oil, salt, ground Szechwan pepper, chili paste, black rice vinegar, and water; set aside.
3. Add oil to a preheated wok or skillet. When oil is hot, add the chopped onion. Stir-fry until soft and translucent.
4. Add the rice noodles and stir-fry for 2 to 3 minutes. Add the sauce in the middle of the wok. Mix in with the noodles and stir-fry until the noodles have absorbed all the sauce.

Burnin' the Midnight Oil

Serve in a chafing dish or in a large table platter. Here's a recipe for homemade hot chili oil: 12 dried red chilies, each about 3 inches long, and ½ pint peanut or corn oil. Remove and discard the seeds from chilies. Chop into flakes and put into a glass jar. Heat the oil in a saucepan until it smokes. Let cool. Pour into jar.

Bow Tie King Crab Salad

Cocktail Complement:

God Bless Texastini
(page 19)

Serves 6

12 ounces bow tie pasta
6 tablespoons olive oil
3 tablespoons lemon juice
2 cloves garlic, minced
Salt to taste
Freshly ground pepper to taste
1 cup fresh king crab
4 scallions, sliced
1 bunch radishes, chopped
2 tablespoons chopped fresh parsley

1. Cook the pasta in water until al dente, then drain.
2. Combine the olive oil, lemon juice, garlic, salt, and pepper. Mix together the crab, scallions, radishes, and parsley.
3. Mix the pasta with the olive oil mixture and let stand 5 minutes. Add the crab mixture, toss again, and serve.

Went to a Garden Party

This is a great dish to serve at a garden party because it's light and airy. Decorate the party with fresh fragrant flowers and candles. You might even send a packet of seeds with your invitations. Hats are popular to wear, too. Decorate with pastels and gauzy materials. You can save money by purchasing sheer curtains at discount stores.

Red Wine Veal Kabobs

Cocktail Complement:

Purple Hooter
(page 126)

Serves 6

1 cup dry red wine

2 tablespoons olive oil

1 teaspoon oregano

1 teaspoon marjoram

1 tablespoon garlic powder

Fresh-cracked black pepper to taste

1 pound veal

2 red bell peppers

2 green Italian peppers

2 yellow bell peppers

1 red onion

1. Soak 12 wooden skewers in water for 4 hours.
2. Mix together the wine, oil, oregano, marjoram, garlic powder, and black pepper. Marinate the veal in this mixture for approximately 1 hour.
3. Preheat grill.
4. Cut the veal into 2-inch cubes. Stem, seed, and quarter the peppers. Cut the onion into wedges.
5. Thread the veal, peppers, and onion (alternating them) onto the skewers and place them on the grill for approximately 2 minutes on all 4 sides.

Cabernet Kabobs

Serve these Red Wine Veal Kabobs on a bed of Wild Almond Apple Rice (page 228). Present it by cutting off the end of a watermelon turned flat side down on a cloth napkin–covered platter. Stick the kabobs in the watermelon piece, then cover the platter with the rice. Lay additional kabobs on the rice.

Pork Apple Casserole

Cocktail Complement:

Grandma's Southern
Blackberry Cobbler
(page 74)

Serves 6

1 apple
1 pear
2 yellow onions
1 stalk celery
1 fennel bulb
½ small head cabbage
1 tablespoon olive oil
1 pound pork
½ teaspoon fennel seeds
½ teaspoon caraway seeds
¼ cup red wine vinegar
1 cup apple or other fruit juice
Fresh-cracked black pepper

1. Preheat oven to 350°F.
2. Dice the apple, pear, and onions. Slice the celery, fennel, and cabbage.
3. Grease a casserole pan with the olive oil. Alternate layers of pork, vegetables, seeds, pepper, vinegar, and juice.
4. Bake, covered, for 45 minutes, then uncover and continue baking for 15 minutes longer. Let cool slightly, then cut and serve.

Comfort Food

If you bake this Pork Apple Casserole in a nice baking dish, you can serve directly from the oven to the serving table. Appetizers that would make a nice combination with the Pork Apple Casserole include the Spiced Pecans (page 148), Fried Coconut Melon (page 167), or Green Apple Salsa (page 155).

Lobster Risotto

Cocktail Complement: Kamikaze (page 122)

Serves 6

1 medium yellow onion
1 shallot
3 cloves garlic
½ bunch parsley
2 teaspoons extra-virgin olive oil
1½ cups Arborio rice
¼ cup dry white wine
3½ cups fish stock
1½ pounds cooked lobster
¼ cup grated Asiago cheese

1. Dice the onion and shallot. Mince the garlic. Chop the parsley.
2. Heat the oil to medium temperature in a medium-size frying pan; sauté the onion for 2 minutes. Add the shallot, and sauté for 1 minute more. Add the garlic, and sauté for 1 more minute.
3. Add the rice and mix well with the sautéed mixture. Pour in the wine and let reduce by half.
4. Add the stock, ½ cup at a time, stirring until each addition is fully incorporated before adding more. Continue the process until all stock is incorporated and the rice is thoroughly cooked.
5. Remove from heat. Stir in the cooked lobster and cheese. Sprinkle with parsley and serve.

Plastic Lobster

This decadent dish can be served on a silver platter on the table if you plan to eat with your guests at a table. If not, it can be kept warm in a buffet-style chafing dish. Look for those big plastic lobsters at party and craft stores to decorate the table.

Turkey Macaroni Casserole

Cocktail Complement:
Cape Cod
(page 120)

Serves 4

½ pound (8 ounces) ground turkey
1 cup chopped onion
1/8 cup (2 tablespoons) unsalted tomato paste
1 teaspoon dried parsley
¼ teaspoon cinnamon
Kosher or sea salt and black pepper to taste
1 cup skim milk
1 tablespoon Ener-G potato flour
2 cups cooked macaroni
4 ounces cheddar cheese, grated (to yield 1 cup)
1 cup béchamel sauce (see sidebar)

1. Preheat oven to 350°F. Fry the ground turkey in a nonstick skillet; drain off any fat and pat the meat with paper towels. Add the onion and sauté with the ground turkey until transparent. Add the tomato paste and sauté until it starts to brown. Stir in the parsley, cinnamon, and salt and pepper, if using. Remove from heat and set aside.
2. Pour the milk in a bowl, add the potato flour, and whisk to mix. Stir in the macaroni and cheese.
3. Treat a 13" × 17" baking dish with nonstick spray. Pour half of the macaroni mixture into the pan. Spread the meat mixture over the macaroni. Add the rest of the macaroni, and top with the béchamel sauce. Bake for 1 hour.

Béchamel Sauce

2 tablespoons butter, 2 tablespoons all-purpose flour, 1 cup heated milk, salt and pepper to taste. Melt butter over medium heat. Add flour and stir. Gradually stir in hot milk. Cook over medium heat, stirring constantly, until sauce begins to boil and thickens. Simmer, stirring frequently, for 5 minutes.

Snappy Ham Ziti

Serves 8

Cocktail Complement:

Cosmopolitan (page 121)

1 16-ounce package ziti pasta

2 tablespoons olive oil

2 cloves garlic, minced

1½ cups sugar snap peas

1½ cups diced cooked extra-lean (4 percent) ham

1 16-ounce can cannellini beans, drained

¼ cup sun-dried tomatoes packed in oil, drained and chopped

1½ cups low-fat, reduced-sodium chicken broth

½ teaspoon kosher or sea salt

¼ teaspoon cracked black pepper

¼ cup grated Parmesan cheese

1. Cook the pasta as directed on the package. Meanwhile, heat a large skillet on medium and add the olive oil. Sauté the garlic for 2 minutes, being careful that it doesn't burn.
2. Add the peas (thawed and drained, if you're using frozen) and stir-fry for about 3 minutes. Stir in the ham, beans, tomatoes, broth, salt, and pepper, and simmer for 5 minutes. Toss the stir-fried bean mixture with the pasta and Parmesan cheese.

Ziti in a Snap

If serving the Snappy Ham Ziti in a chafing dish, don't cook the ziti quite all the way. Present in bowl for a table setting. Appetizers to accompany the Snappy Ham Ziti include Ham Cornets (page 163), Spicy White Bean Sunshine Dip (page 149), or the Spiced Crunchy Okra (page 205).

Thanksgiving Turkey Casserole in a Pumpkin

Cocktail Complement:
Thanksgiving
Turkey Cosmo
(page 104)

Serves 4

4 small pumpkins
1 can cream of chicken soup
1 cup skim milk
1 cup low-fat,
    reduced-sodium chicken broth
1 tablespoon, plus 1 teaspoon butter
½ cup steamed, diced celery
1 cup steamed diced onion
1 cup steamed sliced mushrooms
1 tablespoon cognac (optional)
Parsley, thyme, and
    sage to taste (optional)

1 ⅓ cups cubed
    red potatoes, steamed
½ pound (8 ounces)
    oysters, steamed, chopped
¼ pound (4 ounces)
    cooked turkey, shredded
8 slices day-old bread,
    torn into cubes
2 eggs, beaten

1. Preheat oven to 375°F. Clean the pumpkins, cut off tops, and scrape out the seeds. Put on baking sheet and cover with foil or parchment paper. Bake for 30 minutes, or until the inside flesh is somewhat tender but the pumpkins still retain their shape.
2. While the pumpkins bake, prepare the dressing-style casserole by combining the soup, milk, broth, and butter in a saucepan; stir well to mix and bring to a boil over medium heat. Lower the heat and add the celery, onion, mushrooms, and the cognac and seasonings, if using. Simmer for 3 minutes. Remove from heat and allow to cool slightly.
3. In a large bowl, add the potatoes, oysters, turkey, and bread cubes, and toss to mix.
4. Gradually add the eggs to the soup mixture, whisking the mixture constantly; pour the mixture over the potatoes, meat, and bread cubes. Mix well to coat the bread evenly. Divide the resulting mixture into the four pumpkins. Reduce oven temperature to 350°F and bake for 30 to 40 minutes, or until casserole is firm.

Chicken Ooh La La King

Cocktail Complement:

The Queen Bee Stinger (page 81)

Serves 4

1 can cream of chicken soup

¼ cup skim milk

½ teaspoon Worcestershire sauce

1 tablespoon Hellmann's or Best Foods Real Mayonnaise

¼ teaspoon ground black pepper

2 cups frozen mix of peas and pearl onions, thawed

1 cup frozen sliced carrots, thawed

1 cup sliced mushrooms, steamed

½ pound (8 ounces) cooked chicken, chopped

4 slices whole-wheat bread

1. Combine the soup, milk, Worcestershire, mayonnaise, and pepper in a saucepan and bring to a boil. Reduce heat and add the peas and pearl onions, carrots, mushrooms, and chicken.

2. Simmer until the vegetables and chicken are heated through. Serve over toast.

Serve It Up!

Set a table with plates with doilies or paper napkins on the plates. Purchase a party-store paper gold crown and place on top. The doilies/napkins keep the bowls from slipping on the plates. When ready to serve, place a slice of toast in a bowl. Top toast with the Chicken Ooh La La King, then place the crown on the plate. Ooh la la!

Aloha Casserole

Cocktail Complement:

Blue Hawaiian Punch (page 42)

Serves 4

1 1/3 cups cooked rice

1 medium onion, chopped

1 can cream of celery soup

1 8-ounce can pineapple chunks

¼ cup water

1 teaspoon brown sugar

½ pound lean sliced ham, baked or boiled

Sliced green onions for garnish (optional)

1. Put the rice in a casserole dish and set aside. Place the chopped onion in a covered microwave-safe bowl. Microwave on high until tender, about 1 minute.
2. Add the soup, pineapple with juice, water, and brown sugar to the onion. Heat, covered, on high until the mixture begins to boil, about 1 minute. Stir mixture until the brown sugar is dissolved.
3. Pour half of the soup mixture over the rice. Arrange the ham slices on top of the rice and pour the remaining soup mixture over it. Cover loosely with plastic wrap or a paper towel (to prevent splatters in the microwave) and heat on high until the rice is reheated and ham is warm, about 1 minute.

Free Palm Fronds

If you live in a tropical area, a really inexpensive way to decorate for a Hawaiian luau is to contact a tree-trimming company and ask them for some palm fronds. To save money, simply offer to pick them up at the location of their choice. In most cases you can score them for free.

Stovetop Tuna Casserole

Serves 4

Cocktail Complement:

Watermelon
Tidal Wave
(page 41)

2 cups egg noodles
1 can cream of mushroom soup
1 teaspoon steamed, chopped onion
1 tablespoon steamed, chopped celery
½ cup skim milk
1 ounce American, cheddar, or Colby cheese, shredded (to yield ¼ cup)
1 cup frozen mixed peas and carrots
1 cup steamed, sliced fresh mushrooms
1 can water-packed tuna, drained
4 round bread loaves

1. Cook the egg noodles according to package directions. Drain and return to pan.
2. Add all the ingredients to the pan; stir to blend. Cook over medium heat, stirring occasionally, until the cheese is melted.

Bowling for Tuna

Serve the Stovetop Tuna Casserole in bread bowls. Simply cut off the top of a round bread loaf, keeping this piece. Next hollow out the middle, but make sure that you don't hollow too deep. Scoop the casserole into the bowl and cap with the piece you cut off. The extra hollowed bread can be used for dipping.

Hawaiian Stuffed Macadamia Pork

Cocktail Complement:
Paradise under a Coconut Tree
(page 45)

Serves 8

2½ cups pineapple juice
¼ cup soy sauce
1 tablespoon fresh gingerroot, minced
¼ cup dry white wine
1 tablespoon Madras curry powder
1 teaspoon Thai chili paste or Tabasco sauce, or to taste
1 teaspoon sugar
2 pork tenderloins, about 1½ pounds each
Salt and freshly ground black pepper
1 cup macadamia nuts, coarsely chopped
Fresh parsley, mint, cilantro, and whole macadamia nuts, for garnish

1. In a medium saucepan, mix together the pineapple juice, soy sauce, gingerroot, wine, curry powder, chili paste, and sugar. Bring to a boil and simmer until reduced to 1½ cups.
2. Tunnel holes through the tenderloins using the handle of a knife or a fat knitting needle. The pork tenderloins will become tubes. Salt and pepper the pork, inside and out, pressing into the tube.
3. Stuff in the chopped macadamia nuts and close ends with small metal skewers. Marinate the pork for 1 hour in ½ cup of the pineapple sauce.
4. Set grill to medium.
5. Place pork on grill over indirect heat until the pork is slightly pink inside and brown on the outside. Carve crosswise so that each piece includes some nuts. Serve with the extra pineapple sauce on the side. (Never reuse sauce that has been placed on raw meat.) Garnish with springs of fresh parsley, mint, cilantro, and whole macadamia nuts.

,Hot Italian Sausage Kabobs

Cocktail Complement:

Blue Taboo
(page 86)

Serves 4

1½ pounds Italian sausage
4 green or red Italian frying peppers (thin-skinned)
2 red onions, peeled
2 tablespoons olive oil

1. Parboil the sausages for 10 minutes, then drain them on paper towels and cut into 2-inch chunks.
2. Rinse the peppers and dry on paper towels. Remove the cores and seeds from the peppers. Cut the peppers into large pieces.
3. Cut the onions into quarters, vertically.
4. Thread the sausage, peppers, and onions onto skewers.
5. Preheat the grill to medium, or wait until the coals are ash-covered.
6. Brush the onions and peppers with oil. Grill until the sausages are brown and the vegetables are soft.

Cajun Shrimp Kabobs

Cocktail Complement:

Lemon Love
Shack Shake
(page 93)

Serves 4

1 teaspoon cayenne pepper

1 teaspoon black pepper, freshly ground

1 teaspoon white peppercorns, freshly ground

1 teaspoon pink peppercorns, freshly ground

1 tablespoon garlic powder

1 tablespoon onion powder

½ teaspoon dark brown sugar

1 teaspoon salt

1 teaspoon dried thyme

1½ pounds jumbo shrimp, peeled and deveined

1/3 cup unsalted butter, melted

1. Mix all dry ingredients until well blended. (This spice mix will keep in a closed jar for months at a time.)
2. Preheat the grill to high.
3. Rub some of the pepper mixture into the shrimp; use rubber gloves if you have sensitive hands. Then thread the shrimp onto skewers.
4. Grill, basting with melted butter, for about 2 minutes per side, or until the shrimp are pink.

Spicy Kabobs

To serve the Cajun Shrimp Kabobs, cut off the end of a watermelon and set flat side down on a platter. Display the kabobs stuck all around the watermelon. Lay green curly lettuce on the remainder of the platter then lay the extra kabobs on the lettuce. Also, try the Shrimp Boat Toasts (page 193) as an hors d'oeuvre.

Appendix A:

Additional Resources

Cocktail Party Invitations

Paper Buzz

This is a mother-and-daughter partnership in Lynchburg, Virginia. They carry a large variety of cocktail party invitations.

www.paperbuzz.com

Friends Invited

This invitation company out of Westbury, New York, offers free shipping on all orders.

www.friendsinvited.com

Creations by Leslie

This business is owned by a former Radio City Music Hall Rockette. Her invitations have been featured in many magazines.

www.creationsbyleslie.com

Bar and Cocktail Products

Bar Products

Based in Florida, this company carries the largest selection of bar products on the Internet.

www.barproducts.com

Food Service Direct

This Rhode Island company sells a lot of items, including glasses by the case and even ice molds.

www.foodservicedirect.com

Oriental Trading

This Web site is filled with all kinds of themed party ware that you can purchase in bulk. Use the search option to find almost anything that you need.

www.oriental.com

Free Online Photo Albums

Yahoo!

First sign up for a free account at Yahoo.com. Click the "Photos" link on the home page to begin making your own free photo album. Uploading photos from your computer is easy, and space is unlimited.

www.yahoo.com

Shutterfly

This site provides a nice, free place to upload your photos.

www.shutterfly.com

Photosite

Here's another nice place to upload your digital photos.

www.photosite.com

Appendix B:
The Flavor of Liquor

Not sure where that fruity flavor in your favorite cocktail comes from?
Are you curious about the taste of some of the more exotic-sounding
liquors available? This chart shows you the flavors of a variety of different liquors that are commonly used in mixed drinks.

Liquor	Flavor
Alize Red Passion	Tropical passion fruit
Amaretto	Almond
Applejack	Apple brandy
Blue curaçao (KYOOR-uh-sew)	Orange
Chambord (Sham-BOARD)	Black raspberry
Coffee liqueur	Chocolate coffee
Cointreau (KWAHN-troh)	Orange
Crème do noya (krehm duh ka-NOY-ya)	Almond

Liquor	Flavor
Dark crème de cacao (crème duh ka-KAY-oh)	Chocolate
Drambuie (dram-BOO-ee)	Honey, Scotch whiskey, and herbs
Frangelico	Hazelnut
Goldschlager	Cinnamon
Grand Marnier (marn-YAY)	Orange cognac
Green crème de menthe	Mint
Hpnotiq (hip-NOT-tic)	Tropical fruit
Irish cream liqueur	Irish whiskey, vanilla, and cream
Licor 43	Citrus vanilla
Limoncello	Sweet lemon
Parfait Amour	Orange, vanilla, almond, and rose petals
Passoa (pass-SO-a)	Passion fruit

Liquor	Flavor
Sambuca	Licorice
Sloe gin	Sloeberries
Southern Comfort	Peach-apricot-honey bourbon
Tequila Rose	Strawberry tequila
Tuaca (ta-WAH-ka)	Vanilla-orange-caramel brandy
White crème de cacao	Chocolate
White crème de menthe	Mint

Index

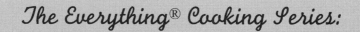

The Everything® Cooking Series:

½ cup delicious recipes
¾ tbsp easy-to-follow instructions
¼ cup value

Mix all together for a tasty treat—
for your mouth, and your wallet!

International Cuisine

The Everything® Chinese Cookbook
1-58062-954-7, $14.95

The Everything® Indian Cookbook
1-59337-042-3, $14.95

The Everything® Italian Cookbook
1-59337-420-8, $14.95

The Everything® Mediterranean Cookbook
1-58062-869-9, $14.95

The Everything® Mexican Cookbook
1-59337-967-9, $14.95

The Everything® Thai Cookbook
1-58062-733-1, $14.95

Beverages

The Everything® Bartender's Book
1-55850-536-9, $9.95

The Everything® Cocktail Parties & Drinks Book
1-59337-390-2, $12.95

The Everything® Wine Book, Completely Updated
1-59337-357-0, $14.95

The Everything® Cooking Series—
Value Tastes Good!

Special Diets

The Everything® Diabetes Cookbook
1-58062-691-2, $14.95

The Everything® Gluten-Free Cookbook
1-59337-394-5, $14.95

The Everything® Healthy Meals In Minutes Cookbook
1-59337-302-3, $14.95

The Everything® Low-Carb Cookbook
1-58062-784-6, $14.95

The Everything® Low-Fat, High-Flavor Cookbook
1-55850-802-3, $14.95

The Everything® Low-Salt Cookbook
1-59337-044-X, $14.95

The Everything® Vegetarian Cookbook
1-58062-640-8, $12.95

General Cooking

The Everything® Barbecue Cookbook
1-58062-316-6, $14.95

The Everything® College Cookbook
1-59337-303-1, $14.95

The Everything® Cookbook
1-58062-400-6, $14.95

The Everything® Cooking for Two Cookbook
1-59337-370-8, $14.95

The Everything® Easy Gourmet Cookbook
1-59337-317-1, $14.95

The Everything® Fondue Cookbook
1-59337-119-5, $14.95

General Cooking (cont)

The Everything® Grilling Cookbook
1-59337-149-7, $14.95

The Everything® Holiday Cookbook
1-59337-129-2, $14.95

The Everything® Meals for a Month Cookbook
1-59337-323-6, $14.95

The Everything® One-Pot Cookbook
1-58062-186-4, $14.95

The Everything® Quick Meals Cookbook
1-58062-488-X, $14.95

The Everything® Slow Cooker Cookbook
1-58062-667-X, $14.95

The Everything® Slow Cooking for a Crowd Cookbook
1-59337-391-0, $14.95

The Everything® Soup Cookbook
1-58062-556-8, $14.95

Available wherever books are sold!
To order, call 1-800-258-0929, or visit us at www.adamsmedia.com.